True stories and true solutions from a survivor of childhood poverty, divorce and abuse

TRIPLE HOOD

THE THREE P'S OF DEALING WITH CHILDHOOD TRAUMA

EUNICE ODERINDE

Published by Brandives
To contact the publisher, please visit:
www.brandives.com or email: brandives.agency@gmail.com

Oderinde, Eunice, author
www.gettriplehood.com
Email: triplehood03@gmail.com

Triple Hood /
ISBN 978 – 1 – 7773270 – 7 – 1

Under a Federal Liberal government, Library and Archives Canada no longer provide Cataloguing in Publication (CIP) data for independently published books.

Editing: Bobbi Beatty, Silver Scroll Services, Calgary, Alberta

DEDICATION

To the victims of childhood sexual abuse,
To the victims of poverty,
To everyone struggling with alcohol and drug misuse,
It is not too late for you to fulfill your purpose in life.
You can overcome your struggles!

Contents

ACKNOWLEDGMENTS

I give glory to God for the grace to birth this vision. I didn't see this project coming.

To all my alpha and beta readers:
Imoleayo Banjo; Bukola Akinwuntan; Tunrayo Adegbenro; Tolani McDonald; Kayode Jegede; Tolu Sajobi; Rachael & Gbenga Owojori, thank you so much for your insightful feedback.

To the editor of this book, Bobbi Beatty, thank you for your professional touch. Your professionalism is top-notch.

A big thank you to Ajibola Olude and Brandives team for the book design and publishing. You're easy to work with.

Pastor Olawumi Oyetuga, thank you for the encouragement.

Pastors Titus & Kunbi Adedapo, thank you for your pastoral support.

To my siblings, Agnes Adeyemi; Sylvester Ogundipe; Cecilia Oyinnijesu; Modupe Adekugbe; Peter Ogundipe; Sunday Adewale; Tobi Israel; Funmilayo Ogundipe; and Omolara Aluko, thank you for your love, help, and counsel.

To my children, Isaac and Esther, thank you for reading the manuscript and for all your suggestions.

To my best friend and husband for life, thank you for the encouragement, prayer, and support throughout every stage of this project.

PREFACE

The wealthiest place in the world is not the gold mines of South America or the oil fields of Iraq or Iran. They are not the diamond mines of South Africa or the banks of the world. The wealthiest place on the planet is just down the road. It is the cemetery. There lie buried companies that were never started, inventions that were never made, bestselling books that were never written, and masterpieces that were never painted. In the cemetery is buried the greatest treasure of untapped potential.[12]

— *Myles Munroe*

Someone who drowns in 7 feet of water is just as dead as someone who drowns in 20 feet of water. Stop comparing traumas, stop belittling you or anyone else's trauma because it wasn't "as bad" as someone else's. This isn't a competition. We all deserve support and recovery[3].

— *Andy Shaw, Mastering The Law of Attraction*

1 Myles Munroe, (2011), *Understanding Your Potential: Discovering the Hidden You,* (Shippensburg, PA: Destiny Image Publishers, 2011).

2 Myles Munroe, *The Wealthy Place Cemetery*, Video file, Accessed February 24, 2022, The Wealthy Place Cemetery- Dr. Myles Munroe- YouTube

3 Mastering Law of Attraction, "The Law of Attraction," Facebook, May 14, 2022, https://www.facebook.com/masteringlawofattraction/

Bayonle stared at the ceiling on and off in the dead of the night. She tossed and turned all night. Despite the mat she had spread on the spring bed hoping it would be somewhat comfortable, it wasn't anywhere near comfortable. It even squeaked every time she rolled over, waking her each time. Bayonle had been poor in elementary school, she had been poor in high school, and now she was poor in college. *When would this end?* As she tried fruitlessly to fall asleep, her mind again flashed back to the day Ola had ejaculated on her when she was just fourteen, to how some of the adult males in her world would touch her inappropriately when she was barely six. Some of the memories made her sick to her stomach. *Why could she not banish these memories? Why were they always there in the darkest part of the night?* As these thoughts swirled around in her mind, she again questioned why she was still alive. She had wished the end would come so many times, yet it never did. *So why was she still here?* Every night would be a repeat of this first night for Bayonle's first few weeks in the hostel she lived in while in college.

One of the incidents that flooded Bayonle's mind as she endured her insomnia that night was her narrow escape from death when she was maybe five years old. *Why didn't I die that day?* she wondered. *I should have. I wouldn't be battered by all these miseries if I had died. I would have transitioned to a better place.* Bayonle's first night in the hostel was miserable. She felt her father had sent her to college to disgrace her. Her tuition had not been paid, and there was no hope it would be paid anytime soon. She had no scholarships, no student loan. *How can a parent send an 18-year-old to college empty handed? This is nothing but a recipe for shame*, she thought.

This was Bayonle's experience, but she isn't alone in her torment.

Let's consider these real-life scenarios.

Judeon, a fifteen-year-old grade ten student, was found lying face down on the floor in his room. When his parents asked his sister to go call him to come for dinner, she discovered him motionless on the floor. She screamed when he didn't wake up despite how loud she yelled his name and how hard she shook his lifeless body. His parents rushed upstairs, called the emergency number, and performed CPR. Unfortunately, Judeon was long gone; the paramedics pronounced him dead upon their arrival. What a tragedy! It turned out he had experimented with illicit drugs with the hope it would boost his confidence as he suffered from low self-esteem.

Judeon had wanted to be an aeronautical engineer when he grew up. His dream was aborted. His flower faded in an untimely fashion. His parents won't see him graduate from high school or college; they wouldn't see him get married or meet their grandchildren. What a wasted destiny!

***

Toyany was a final-year college student when the unspeakable happened. She overdosed and died before her time. She had wanted to be a pediatrician. She was twenty-four.

***

Prudent was twenty-seven when his life was cut short. He had started experimenting with booze in his early teens. He could not control his appetite for alcohol and suffered irreversible liver damage. Upon his death, multiple organs had shut down. He was an up-and-coming chef at the time.

Now I'm not suggesting death is the only consequence of substance misuse. The majority of users, though they live, do not make good, healthy choices. This is simply due to the effects drugs have on the brain. Some people can't function appropriately in society; some inflict injuries on themselves and others. Destinies are being shattered by the continuous engagement in this destructive lifestyle brought into being by people's need to cope.

Let's look at a few more scenarios.

Linax is thirty-eight. His parents were teenagers when they had him. They were high-school sweethearts. His mother dropped out of high school when she discovered she was pregnant with him. His father continues to pursue his dreams and ambition. Unfortunately, his parents broke up: no engagement, no wedding. A few years later, his parents went their separate ways without looking back.

Linax's life turned upside down, and his relationship with his parents became nothing to write home about. No father figure in his life, no role model. So Linax turned to alcohol for comfort. He couldn't control his appetite for booze. People often found him passed out in odd places after a few shots of drink. At thirty-eight, he had no family, no education, no trade, and no job.

***

Pat was an ambitious young girl growing up. She wanted to be a lawyer. Unfortunately, the trauma of her childhood robbed her of the prosperous life she had envisioned. She was verbally, emotionally, and physically abused by the man she called her dad. Relatives and neighbours abused her sexually. She was damaged going into her adult life. Between the ages of fourteen and eighteen, she'd had four abortions. Pat wanted male affirmation so bad that she could not maintain a stable relationship. She moved from one man to the next like someone trying on clothes to see what fits. Her memory of her father is of a servant-master relationship. Her father cursed her at every slight mistake; he dehumanized her by calling her horrible names; he publicly disgraced her, including in the presence of her school peers.

Let's get something straight: traumatic life experiences are not the only reason people use drugs and alcohol or become promiscuous. The genesis of many people's substance abuse can also be prescription drugs, chronic illness, untreated severe mental illness, and more. But this is not what this book is about.

Drug misuse and substance abuse is on the rise worldwide. News of increased overdoses and deaths are becoming more common than in previous decades. According to a study conducted by Ritchie and Roser in 2019, 11.8 million people per year died across the globe due to smoking, alcohol abuse, and illicit drug use.[4] In Canada, over 26,000 people died of illicit drug overdoses between 2016 and 2021. That number increased by 95 percent in the first year of the COVID-19 pandemic.[5] That's an incredible jump from 2016. Are there workable strategies one can adopt to live a substance-free life in this present day and age?

Nearly every day as Bayonle watches the news, she

4 Hannah Ritchie and Max Roser, "Drug Use," *Our World In Data,* December 2019, https://ourworldindata.org/drug-use.

5 Government of Canada, *Opioid and Stimulant-Related Harms in Canada,* June 2022 https://health-infobase.canada.ca/substance-related-harms/opioids-stimulants/

reminisces about her childhood. Yes, she had it rough! Being raised by a single parent is one thing; experiencing abuse is entirely another.

From her early childhood to adulthood, poverty beat her up at night; misogyny stared her down in the morning. It was hard for her to get out of bed. Depression became her shroud, pushing her into isolation as she hid deeper within herself, afraid of the rest of the world. Bayonle was abused sexually, emotionally, and physically by relatives and acquaintances. There were nights she would wish she would close her eyes and never wake up to see the break of the next day. She wanted everything to end in the twinkle of an eye.

And yet she overcame; she survived. So what were Bayonle's coping mechanisms throughout her struggles?

You have many Toyanys and Linaxes as your neighbours, colleagues, family members, and acquaintances. They're haunted by their past. Every one of them has their own story. They're hurting, and some turn to alcohol and or drugs to help "take the edge off." Perhaps they thought it would be a one-time deal, but then they got hooked. It was a journey of no return. Does this resonate with you? The irony is, no one can tell another's reason(s) for using alcohol or illicit drugs just by looking at them. This book addresses some of the bad experiences, trauma, and misfortunes endured early in life that could push one to a lifestyle of drug and substance abuse.

The journey to healing is different from person to person; however, the optimal goal is freedom. Every victim of trauma deserves a full recovery and freedom from torment. Everyone struggling with addiction deserves support and a full recovery. Bayonle's escape route is a unique one that I believe victims of childhood sexual abuse, parental divorce, and poverty would benefit from.

Preface

This book is a true-life story, and the scenarios are real-life experiences. Some are from family, friends, or acquaintances; some are from the news. But all are real. However, names and personal information have been modified to preserve anonymity.

PART 1

PREVENTION

1

A Baby Girl is Born

Bayonle is the youngest of Anthonia and Michael's three daughters. She was fondly called daddy's girl. This is partly because Michael would take her wherever he went when she wasn't in school. Unfortunately, she used this privilege of being close to her dad to her advantage. She was a snitch! She got her sisters in trouble many times and got away with so many things. As a result, Bayonle's relationship with her sisters wasn't the greatest. Every time she told on them, Michael would punish them. This created tension between her and her sisters. Eventually, they would not discuss anything they didn't want Michael to hear when she was around. That made Bayonle feel isolated. But who could blame her sisters? Looking back, she attributes her attitude toward her sisters as lack of social skills. Does this resonate with you?

Bayonle knew how to get whatever she wanted from her father. Michael was eighty-three when Bayonle was born. Eighty-three! Being his last child—and perhaps because she was born in his old age—he treated her differently than he did her sisters. Bayonle doesn't remember him beating her. Verbal reprimands she recalls, yes, but not physical punishments. All Bayonle's siblings knew Michael had a soft spot for her. But you will read about their father-daughter relationship throughout this book.

One display of Bayonle's boldness happened when she was about ten years old. Michael wanted to travel to their hometown with Bayonle. Alas! Bayonle blatantly refused. Defiance was unheard of. None of her siblings ever did that, not when they were ten and not when they were twenty. They would not, could not, go against Michael's orders or confront him. He would beat them black and blue if they talked back. Let's boil this down to its true essence: their opinions never mattered to him.

When Bayonle was eleven, she stole Mope, her stepmother's money. When Mope confronted her about it, she denied it. Michael took Bayonle's word over his wife's. Mope brought in a third party to testify to Bayonle's delinquency; still, Michael wouldn't budge despite all the evidence Mope presented.

Let's rewind and look at the past, at the circumstances of Bayonle's birth and her parents' lives to gain a deeper understanding of their lives, experiences, decisions, and consequences.

December 1975

It was a Sunday during the dry season in Nigeria, West Africa. Dry leaves lay strewn over the ground as they effortlessly fell off the trees. The soft crunching sound as one walks in the park is gratifying. The harmattan cold was mild that day. Harmattan season in Nigeria is between November and March and is when the dry and dusty northeasterly wind blows from the Sahara over West Africa.

The day started with cold temperatures but warmed in the afternoon. According to Anthonia, Bayonle's birth was a normal delivery. There were no complications. Anthonia's labour started in the morning and by late afternoon, her beautiful, chubby, healthy baby girl was born. Anthonia heaved a sigh of relief as she watched the midwife cut the cord. Her vision became blurry as tears ran down her cheeks. She quickly wiped her face when the midwife asked if everything was okay. Her pregnancy journey had been an emotional rollercoaster.

Anthonia was terribly sick during her pregnancy—and scared. She wasn't sure what the outcome of her illness combined with her pregnancy would be. It had started with a dry, irritating cough, then it progressed into chest pain and difficulty breathing. She used every home remedy she knew with no relief. Finally, Anthonia had no choice but to go to the hospital. Her worst nightmare became a reality when the doctor told her the diagnosis. It was tuberculosis (TB). She was terrified she would lose her baby. The next few months would be the most challenging period for her.

The stress of going to the health centre daily for anti-TB injections for four weeks was nerve-racking. Being pregnant is one challenge, but fighting to overcome illness while pregnant is quite another. And she also had to care for her older children and her home while fighting her illness every day. Nonetheless, she endured the difficult time knowing everything would be all right once she held her baby in her arms.

The first two weeks after the delivery was also challenging. Anthonia could hardly stay awake. She dozed off while breastfeeding her baby. It was hard to concentrate as she would tire easily. She was mentally and emotionally drained. Thankfully, a few weeks later, Anthonia's immediate older sister, Abi, came to support her. Abi did all the chores and bathed the baby. The only thing Anthonia was allowed to do during the few weeks Abi stayed with them was eat and breastfeed the baby. This act of kindness from Abi allowed Anthonia to rest and take care of herself. Perhaps without this blessed intervention, Bayonle's childhood would have been even more difficult.

The name "Bayonle" means "meet joy at home." So while her name was coined from joy, would she meet joy at home? Did she experience joy growing up?

We will see later in the book.

Michael

Michael Osho Ogundipe was born in 1892 in Ekiti State, Nigeria. His parents and older siblings were farmers who specialized in cocoa plantation. So, Michael grew up mastering the nitty-gritty of cocoa farming. Unfortunately, rumours of infidelity on the part of Michael's mother, Kuku, circulated around the time she was pregnant with Michael. They claimed that her husband, Okutu, wasn't Michael's father. But Okutu turned a deaf ear to these rumours. He protected Kuku and raised Michael like his other children. His older siblings and their friends would bully and assault him whenever Okutu wasn't around. Michael couldn't tell Okutu about his siblings' attitude toward him in Okutu's absence; his siblings had threatened to kill him if he did. So he continued to endure physical and emotional abuse from his siblings. Finally in his early adult years, Michael decided to find a way to escape the abuse.

Michael's greener pasture was a job in the home of a forest guard, Fadele. A forest guard is a government employee that stops illegal deforestation. Michael worked as a houseboy for Fadele for a few years until a job in road construction came up. Then he became part of the crew that constructed one of the Nigerian state roads. It was working this job that he learned how to read and write. He worked during the day and went to reading-and-writing class in the evening. When the road construction was complete in 1929, Michael relocated to Oyo State, where he continued to do menial jobs. His plan was to save up enough money to get married and start a family. Unfortunately, his income from his menial jobs didn't cut it. As a result, Michael thought about learning a trade.

In 1936, Michael decided he would be a goldsmith. He went to learn from one of the best in the trade. He was dedicated and became very skillful before he completed his training. Michael's excellence in the trade was such that customers started to prefer his service over his mentor's. After his goldsmith training, he met a beautiful woman named Ebun. They dated for a few months and later tied the knot in 1940.

Michael and Ebun's marriage lasted only four years. Ebun went to court and got a divorce. She claimed Michael was impotent despite having a son together and being pregnant with their second child when she left Michael. There was no DNA testing back then. The court believed Ebun's testimony that she was impregnated twice by another man while married to Michael. This was the first of his five failed marriages.

Anthonia

Anthonia Aladejana was born in 1942 in Ekiti State. Her father had many wives, and Anthonia's mother was one of his favourite wives. This rubbed off on Anthonia as her father was also fond of her. Unfortunately, this happiness was short-lived. Her parents divorced in her early teens, and her father died in her late teens. The divorce and the death of her father resulted in her living with relatives. As a result, Anthonia did not enjoy stability growing up. She also experienced her share of poverty and emotional abuse. Although she wanted to earn a higher education, it did not come to pass as she moved from one relative's house to another. Moreover, her family simply couldn't afford it. In the end, she only completed an elementary education.

Anthonia decided to learn a trade in her early adult years. She chose sewing. At just twenty-two, Anthonia dated a teacher named Mr. Ade while she was in training to be a seamstress. Anthonia and Mr. Ade had a boy named Mide. Although Anthonia became pregnant a few months into their relationship, sadly, no marriage came of it. Anthonia's relatives didn't like Mr. Ade. They threatened him day after day, saying things like, "You're not good enough for our sister. She's a princess. You'll be in big trouble if you don't leave our sister alone." After a while, Mr. Ade couldn't take it anymore; he got frustrated and left town. The pregnancy came to be the deal-breaker. Apparently, Mr. Ade didn't want to be on the bad side of Anthonia's family, so he chose to keep his life and sanity. The next thing Anthonia heard about Mr. Ade was that he had passed away. Mide was only a toddler when Mr. Ade died.

Anthonia was devastated by Mr. Ade's death. He had

been Anthonia's first love, and her family robbed her of the opportunity to be with him. The fact that her son would grow up without a father made Anthonia fearful. She no longer had a good relationship with some of her relatives because they disapproved of her relationship with Mr. Ade, so she was faced with a terrible challenge. All Anthonia had ever experienced from her childhood on was one challenge after another.

In 1968, Anthonia and Michael met and married. It was Michael's third marriage. You'll learn more about Anthonia and Michael's relationship in the next chapter.

2

The Divorce

Marriage is a journey into the unknown. You think you know everything about your spouse, but you will spend each day unravelling them.
— Eunice Oderinde

According to Anthonia, her marriage with Michael was not what she had expected. Michael constantly accused her of infidelity. Moreover, he was controlling. They argued over every little thing, and when she couldn't take it anymore, she called it quits. She was torn between staying for the sake of her children and leaving for her sanity.

The age difference between Anthonia and Michael might have contributed to why they didn't see eye to eye on many things. The decision to marry Michael wasn't Anthonia's but that of the community elders. Before Anthonia came into the picture, Michael was still married to his second wife, although they were "separated," and he already had seven children. Even with no attraction, no love, and no dating, young Anthonia had to obey the elders. Their argument was Michael would take good care of her because he was fifty years older than her. No wonder the couple wasn't on the same page on most things. It seemed she couldn't do anything right as far as her relationship with Michael was concerned. Despite her best efforts, there was always unresolved tension between them.

Her decision made, their divorce was made even more painful because she knew her three children would never be the same. She felt hurt, disappointed, and betrayed by the elders. Anthonia decided she was done! She vowed not to allow anyone to dictate how to run her love life and relationships ever again. "I was blind, but now I see" was how Anthonia felt when her marriage with Michael went south. She may have been naïve at the beginning of their relationship, but after having three children with Michael, she now knew better.

The age gap wasn't the couple's only challenge; they also had a blended family. Anthonia has never said much about her relationship with her stepchildren. Four of her step children were adults and had already left home either for college or work in another city when Anthonia and Michael got married. The youngest three were between four and fifteen at the time. The fifteen-year-old looked after her two younger siblings, so Anthonia really didn't have much of a relationship with them. Michael's previous divorce had pushed his youngest children to grow up fast and take on adult responsibilities like chores and cooking. The lack of a bond between Anthonia and her stepchildren surely could not have helped matters.

Bayonle was a toddler when Anthonia and Michael ended their marriage. Anthonia was even still breastfeeding Bayonle, so she went with Anthonia when she left Michael. Bayonle's older siblings were seven and four years old, so Anthonia left them in Michael's custody. When she later married one of her admirers, Anthonia's mother offered to take Bayonle to live with her in another state so Anthonia could have more time to devote time to her new lover. What are mothers for after all?!

As Anthonia says, although it was painful for her, she felt she had to send Bayonle to live with her mother for her new marriage to work. That became another of the toughest decisions Anthonia had ever had to make.

Bayonle's grandma was well-known in her community because of her career. She was an herbalist. Her fame attracted guests to her house on a regular basis, and they would bring her candies and biscuits. It's common practice in the Yoruba culture for guests to bring goodies for their host's children. Regrettably, some of these people would caress young Bayonle. Day after day and month after month, she became used to the gifts and the touch of the guests. Eventually, it didn't bother her. It was all she knew.

But then the severity of the occurrences began to increase. Many times, Bayonle would find herself pinned to the couch in her living room by a neighbourhood teenager. He would threaten her and say she would be in big trouble if she told. To Bayonle, that was the normal way of playing with older males; at least, that was what she was told. It was only when she became older that she realized that the males who touched her inappropriately took advantage of her innocence for their sexual pleasure. It was not normal, or okay.

Does this resonate with you?

3

Stop Touching Me!

When two elephants fight, the grass suffers.
—African proverb

Bayonle remembers being touched inappropriately by male relatives and acquaintances. To her five- to nine-year-old self, this was the norm. The female adults around her would make matters worse by calling Bayonle "the wife" of these male figures. This made her felt special. To them it was just a joke, but psychologically, they were unintentionally helping in the grooming. She doesn't remember being instructed by any adults around her to not allow anyone to touch certain parts of her body. So, I'm telling you now in case no one has ever told you either. Private parts should stay private. Are you a victim of sexual abuse? You need to speak up to advocate for your own healing process, and to help others. But the right time to speak up is determined by you. You know yourself more than anyone knows you; it's important that you say something to someone **when you're ready.** You will know the right time to do this.

***

Another innocent child who experienced sexual abuse was

Ngozi, one of Bayonle's friends. She was constantly abused sexually by her father's friend and her domestic staff. Ngozi's parents were business moguls. Their chain of businesses took them away from home most of the time. They depended on domestic staff, family, and friends to watch their children when they were gone. Their "trusted" friend and domestic staff took advantage of Ngozi's parents' absence and abused her sexually. What a shame! The driver that took her to school started touching her at the age of six. Then when she was going through puberty, the driver would fondle her breasts in the car all the way to her school and back. When her parents saw she was struggling in math, they hired one of her father's childhood friends to tutor her three times a week. Three months in, the teacher had groomed Ngozi to perform oral sex on him. This happened when the other domestic staff were gone on errands. The math teacher knew her parents' schedules and the staff's schedules. He molested her at least once a week when no one was home. She couldn't tell anyone about it as the predator had threatened to hurt her, her parents, and himself.

With time, Ngozi started having sex with boys in her school. She received no positive affirmation from her father as he was always away, so she unconsciously searched for approval from any male. As a result, any male who said nice things to her could sleep with her if they know how to play their cards right. By the time she turned seventeen, she'd had three abortions. Ngozi is now in her 50s and on a journey to healing, but her past still haunts her every now and then. She wishes she had run away from home or told someone.

***

A child wants to be loved, not violated. Predators look for

young children to satisfy their inordinate affection. They're pedophiles and they know their game. They use their cunning strategies to win the trust of innocent children.

Most parents do their best to protect their children from predators. Unfortunately, some parents miss the signs. This is partly because some were victims of sexual abuse and molestation. Some of these adults are so traumatized and broken that they normalize the inappropriate behaviour they witness in their children. Studies have shown that 30 percent of abuse victims will abuse their children. And for other parents, their nonchalant attitude is simply ignorance. Since they didn't experience good parenting growing up, they struggle with being good parents for their children. They can't give what they don't have. They are emotionally damaged, and they need help themselves.[6]

As with other children who are victims of abuse, the darkness that surrounded Bayonle, a poor lonely child, was scary. Bayonle's darkness was so immense and unrelenting that she lost her inner sight. She often felt hopeless, helpless, and confused. We need to understand that children don't have the same sense of reasoning as adults; their brains are still developing. They are vulnerable; they can be groomed for abuse easily. Parental love is one of the fundamental needs of a child. If this is lacking, the child will accept affection from anyone ready to provide it. Even more important is parental presence. Bayonle longed for her mother. Children whose parents are

6 Noll, Jennie G., Penelope K. Trickett, William W. Harris, and Frank W. Putnam, "The Cumulative Burden Borne by Offspring Whose Mothers Were Sexually Abused as Children: Descriptive Results From A Multigenerational Study," *Journal of Interpersonal Violence*, 24, no. 3 (March 2009.): 424–449. National Library of Medicine. https://doi.org/10.1177/0886260508317194

absent or not active are prone to accepting attention from anyone, including predators and pedophiles.

It's important that parents and guardians teach children under their care sex education. Children need to learn about their body parts and the importance of not allowing anyone to touch them inappropriately. The danger of a lack of sex education is grievous. Abuse victims may grow up to accept the abuse as a normal way of life and become pedophiles in training. Studies have shown that 40 percent of pedophiles were sexually abused in their childhood.

Equally, studies revealed increased rates of mental illness, suicidal thoughts, suicidal attempts, alcohol, and illicit drug abuse among childhood sexual abuse survivors.[7] Perhaps the adults in little Bayonle's life didn't know they were digging a pit for her. Perhaps they too were abuse victims. Either way, she had no choice but to live the hand she'd been dealt.

7 Fergusson, David M., Geraldine F. H. McLeod, and L. John Horwood, "Childhood sexual abuse and adult developmental outcomes: Findings from a 30-year longitudinal study in New Zealand." *Child Abuse & Neglect,* 37, no. 9 (2013): 664-674. Childhood sexual abuse and adult developmental outcomes: Findings from a 30-year longitudinal study in New Zealand

4

The Relocation

While Bayonle lived with her grandma, her two older sisters lived with Michael. She wasn't even ten when she left her grandma to reunite with Michael and her sisters. Bayonle's immediate older sister, Omolara, had come to stay with Bayonle and their grandma during school break, and Michael had told Omolara to talk Bayonle into coming to live with them. Fortunately, it worked!

Bayonle didn't have any recollection of her sisters because her parents had divorced when she was a toddler, and she had been separated from her sisters. Part of her was excited because she would live with her father and siblings; and part of her was sad. She would miss her grandma, her aunt, her neighbourhood friends, her school friends, and her teacher, Mrs. Oguntuyi. Despite the abuse, Bayonle did have some fond memories of her early childhood with her grandma.

There was no internet, no social media, and no television during Bayonle's early childhood years. Children played with mud, grass, and old vehicle tires back then. They would cook imaginary food with tin cans as pots. The adults would gather children together in the front yard or the backyard in the evening for storytelling. This was done under the moonlight all year round in Nigeria. The weather was favourable for outdoor play as there was no snow and no extremely cold temperatures.

Bayonle loved to listen to the stories.

Another of her favourite memories of her time with her grandma included the games she would play with the children and the games she would play with her grandma. One of Bayonle's favourite children's games was "ten-ten." This game is played with two kids facing each other. As the lead sings ten-ten, they both hop and clap. It is similar to Rock, Paper, Scissors. The only difference is that each kid will put one foot forward—instead of a hand—as they stomp with the other one. The game helped kids focus, learn numbers, and build their speed and strategic reasoning.

Bayonle loved to play board games with her grandma. She learned how to play *ayo olopon,* an African board game, and another board game called *ludo* before she left her grandma's place. These two games were her grandma's favourites, and she gradually influenced Bayonle to fall in love with them. As young as she was, she became a threat to other players in the neighbourhood because her grandma had taught her the tricks of the game so well.

***

By the time Bayonle moved in with Michael, he had married another woman. Bayonle's new stepmom had a boy named Telax from her previous marriage. He was in his late teens when Bayonle met him. Telax would later become Bayonle's worst nightmare. But let's back up a bit.

Michael was a workaholic. Bayonle can't remember a single day that he missed work. He would go to his goldsmith shop six days a week: Monday to Saturday. After school, she would go to the shop with her sisters until closing time. The shop didn't have a consistent closing time, however. Sometimes

Michael wouldn't even close for the day until 8:30 p.m.

This was perfect for Telax, because he used Michael's attitude toward work to his own advantage. Telax would ask Bayonle to come home with him on those nights Michael kept the shop open late. Even beyond those days, her stepbrother would always find an excuse, a way to get Bayonle alone with him in the house. His only aim was to touch her inappropriately. He insisted it was a "do-not-tell" affair, a special secret.

Unfortunately and fortunately, this marriage was short-lived. It lasted only about three years; with the end of the marriage came the end of Telax and Bayonle's unhealthy relationship. But the damage had already been done. The seed of lust had been planted and was starting to grow in Bayonle's heart. She felt like damaged goods. Who would rescue her from this mess?

Researchers have linked depression to poor social skills.[8] Bayonle suffered in silence as she watched her social life ruined by her traumatic childhood experience. She was always sad and irritable. She often held grudges against neighbours. She lacked motivation, felt guilty about things she did or didn't do, and had suicidal thoughts. How would she ever navigate through life successfully? Bayonle felt like no one wanted her. She was convinced that she had been born into this world only to suffer. Whenever she was sick with malaria, the common cold, or laryngitis, she would wish it would kill her so she could escape from her life of sexual abuse and poverty. Loneliness and isolation encapsulated her.

8 Segrin, Chris, "Social skills deficits associated with depression," *Clinical Psychology Review*, 20, no. 3 (April 2000): 379-403, Retrieved May 18, 2022, from https://www.sciencedirect.com/science/article/abs/pii/S0272735898001044

A Snapshot of Bayonle's Home Environment

To really understand Bayonle requires a complete visual of where and how she lived during her formative years after she left her grandmother. During her elementary and high-school years, Bayonle lived in an overcrowded two-storey house with her family. Her family did not occupy both floors. Instead, there were twelve rooms on the second floor, and six families lived on this floor alone. The average size of each family was four people. Bayonle's family occupied just two rooms. One room was the living room and the children's room. The children have their bed in the living room. They shared one double bed—a spring bed with an old, brown mattress—that occupied the space against the wall opposite the door. They all slept on that same bed for more than two decades. Bayonle doesn't remember the bed having a fabric cover either. As far back as she could remember, the mattress was always bare and it certainly was not white. They even had to spray it periodically to eliminate bedbugs. At the foot of the tattered bed was a clothes rack. By the window was an old, sagging sofa, and across from that were two armchairs, a small, brown wooden table centred between them. Against the wall across from the sitting area was a big table, upon which sat a record player with which Michael played his favourite artist: Adedara Arounralojaoba. Under the table was the "pantry." Cooked food, plates, and utensils occupied a 30" × 15" light-green cupboard by the door, and a 45" × 25" mahogany storage shelf beside that stored all their books and papers. That one room was where Bayonle spent much of her life.

The hallway in front of each tenant's room was the "kitchen," which included only a table, cooking pots, utensils, and a kerosene stove. They didn't have luxury kitchen appliances like the refrigerators and dishwashers that rich families had.

The second room was solely Michael's.

All the tenants on the second floor shared one bathroom. There was always a long queue on weekdays and Sundays. There were only two toilets—one for each floor—and they were both on the main floor.

Bayonle's favourite spot in the house was the second-floor balcony. The house was on the main road right across from her elementary school. She didn't have to walk long distances to school like some other children, so at least she had that. She was also fortunate that her high school was located behind her elementary school. The two schools were only separated by a high fence.

The balcony became a den or rec room for all the tenants, adults and children alike. Bayonle liked watching pedestrians, vehicles, motorbikes, and food vendors go by. Most times, people didn't even have to go to the market to buy groceries. Instead, if one stayed about an hour on the balcony, one could buy everything needed to make dinner. Most beef vendors used bicycles with a carrier—and made good use of their bike horns. The horns were so loud that people could hear them from their rooms. All people needed to do was to wave a vendor down from the balcony and run outside to buy their meat. It was the same for other food items; families could buy most things from the comfort of the balcony.

Bayonle does have some good memories of lounging in the safety and comfort of that balcony. She loved watching all the special events that would take place on the street. For instance, after she graduated from elementary school, she would watch the school's sports day from the balcony, and during summer break, she would watch the parties people held; folks would actually rent the school field for their parties. One such party was the performance of a renowned artist from the east.

Bayonle watched from the balcony with the other kids.

The scenery and the distractions from the balcony nearly got Bayonle into big trouble with Michael one Saturday morning. Moses was a teenager that lived with his parents on the main floor. Moses was a fearless boy who liked to experiment. He took a few shots of his father's aromatic schnapps, and an hour later became an entertainer.

Everyone watched him from the balcony. At that time, Bayonle was frying *akara* (bean cake). As she was standing watching Moses's one-man drama as if hypnotized, she suddenly remembered she hadn't tasted the *akara*. She quickly checked—and thank God too because it hadn't yet burned. As she was about to put the last batch in the hot oil, she tasted one of the cakes—and realized she hadn't added salt. So, she added salt to the last batch before she fried it. Knowing the morning would not be a good one if she had served Michael tasteless *akara*, she was relieved she'd caught it in time. The rest of them would have to eat a tasteless breakfast, however.

The Olusolas were Bayonle's second-floor neighbours. Mr. Olusola was an elementary school teacher, while Mrs. Olusola was a petty trader. They were the first family on the floor to buy a television. Their long TV antenna was attached to the balcony rail, and they would have to adjust it periodically to get good reception.

Their living room was usually packed full during soccer season, especially during the World Cup tournament. The adults sat around the dining table and on the two sofas, while children sat on the floor. Every now and then, you could hear people screaming, "It's a goooal!" when their favourite team scored and, "Oh noooo!" if they missed a shot. Some folks would get really into it and put their hands on their head and stand very close to the TV in anticipation of a goal. Of course, fans of the winning team would always taunt those of the losing team.

No one could take a nap when the games were on. If their team won, the adults would embrace and shake hands, while the children would jump up and down through the whole house. They would chant, "*O se, o se o, o se o, o se, Baba,*" meaning "Thank you, thank you, thank you, thank you, Father." Mr. Olusola would then play his favourite artists' records: Sir Shina Peters, Bob Marley, King Sunny Ade, and Michael Jackson. The noise from the Olusolas' would wake even a deep sleeper in no time. Bayonle wasn't a big sports fan, but she liked to watch TV series and soaps at the Olusolas'.

Mrs. Olusola was fond of Bayonle. She always said that every day Bayonle was the first person to buy items from her, then that day would be a big sales' day. Subsequently, Mrs. Olusola cultivated a routine of giving Bayonle money in the evening to buy biscuits or other snacks from her the next morning. This singular act made Bayonle feel good about herself. Although she didn't consider herself a superstitious person, she thought of the "good luck" she brought to Mrs. Olusola's business as more than a mere coincidence. Was it a sign she had good fortunes inside her after all? She reflected on this many times. Maybe eventually, her future could be great.

Unfortunately, a troubled young adult lived in the same house. His name was Ola. He lived with his brother, Mr. Folahan, for about three years while he completed high school. He had been struggling in school in his hometown, so his family had decided he should go live with Mr. Folahan, who was a teacher. Ola was eighteen; Bayonle was just fourteen at the time. Ola would always brag to her about how he was sleeping with other girls in their neighbourhood. This was his way of sensitizing her. He would often come to her room to seduce her when no one was home. He would expose himself in front of her, and he ejaculated on her twice. He even attempted to rape her three times. The third time, her adrenaline soared! She was ready to fight her way to freedom. She determined to put an end to Ola's lustful behaviour. She left a bite mark on his left cheek as she pushed him to the floor. Does this resonate with you?

Though Bayonle tried to keep Ola's lustful behaviour a secret for a while, she finally reached a point where she couldn't hold it in anymore. It felt like she was about to explode. But she couldn't tell her father. First, she feared raising the alarm would come back to bite her somehow. Second, she felt he would blame her. Bayonle would discover much later that the fear of being blamed for being the cause of sexual abuse has kept many, many victims mute.[9] [10]

Finally, after being hesitant for so long, Bayonle confided in Mrs. Olusola. She told the older woman of the bite mark on Ola's cheek. It was evidence of Bayonle's truthfulness. Mrs. Olusola confronted him, and he could not deny it. That was the end of him sexually exploiting Bayonle. To her, this was a triumph. At last, she was strong enough to fight for herself and speak up. Although Mrs. Olusola wasn't an attorney or an authority figure, Bayonle had still found her voice through her.

Michael travelled to their hometown quarterly, leaving Bayonle in the care of neighbours, though she still slept in

9 Child Exploitation and Online Protection Centre (CEOP), "Why don't children tell their parents about sexual abuse?" Retrieved May 18, 2022, from https://www.thinkuknow.co.uk/parents/articles/Why-dont-children-tell-their-parents-about-sexual-abuse/

10 Watkins-Kagebein, Jennifer, Barnett, T. M., Collier-Tenison, S., and Blakey, J, "They Don't Listen: A Qualitative Interpretive Meta-Synthesis of Children's Sexual Abuse," Child and Adolescent Social Work Journal, 36, no. 4 (August 15, 1999): 337-349.

her own room when her father wasn't in town. After the incident with Ola, she became more cautious of her security. She would double-check that the door and the windows were locked before she went to bed. Then she would wake up in the middle of the night to check again. Bayonle didn't want anything to jeopardize her dreams of going to post-secondary school. From what she knew, pregnancy would mean the end of her education. She had seen teenage mothers in the neighbourhood, and that's the last thing she wanted to be. She just couldn't see herself pregnant at that stage of her life. So, she avoided boys like the plague for a few years. Does this resonate with you?

***

Bukky, an acquaintance of Bayonle was fifteen when two armed men approached her around 10 p.m. on her way home from her mother's grocery store. It was late at night, the world was dark, and there were no streetlights on; there had been a power outage. One of the men put a knife to her throat and threatened to kill her if she made noise, while the other one covered her face with a blindfold. They carried her to a nearby bush and raped her. Bukky did not tell her parents—or anyone else. She even had an aunt that was a registered nurse in their local hospital who could have easily taken her to the emergency room for a rape kit, but Bukky didn't tell her either. She thought no one would believe her.

Bukky lived with this trauma; she suffered in silence for a long time. She became withdrawn and would stay in her room for long hours on weekends. She skipped school or would leave the house in the morning at the same time as her younger sister, who was in elementary school. When Bukky just couldn't face school, she would skip and go to an uncompleted building near her house. There, she would hide for a couple hours, waiting for her parents to go to work before she would run back home. Initially, her parents thought she was acting weird due to puberty, but over time, her symptoms became psychosomatic. She suffered constant headaches, lost weight due to her poor appetite, and endured awful abdominal pain. Her parents eventually took her to the hospital after they had tried all they could at home without success. When Bukky was diagnosed with depression, her parents couldn't put their finger on why their daughter was depressed. Finally, after a lot of digging by a psychiatrist and some therapists, the truth came out. It was tragic, but it was a relief for her parents to finally know the origin of Bukky's malady.

That relief was short-lived. They were confused. They thought they were good parents, and they struggled to understand why their daughter wouldn't come to them when she was troubled. After some self-reflection, they saw a few lapses in their parenting style and decided to fix them.

Research has shown that 53 percent to 55 percent of victims of child sexual abuse don't tell their parents because they are ashamed and embarrassed. Some children don't know how or when to talk about the abuse. Some believe nothing can be done about it, so why tell someone?[11] In Bukky's case, she was blindfolded and raped by strangers, so she was sure she would not recognize them to identify them. So, why tell when nothing can be done about it? Does this resonate with you?

Then There Are Mommy Issues

There were things Bayonle believed she could have been very good at if her mother, Anthonia, had been in the picture.

11 Child Exploitation and Online Protection Centre (CEOP).

Motherly advice and guidance would have helped Bayonle better navigate puberty. There are so many things girls learn from their mothers that Bayonle missed out on because she didn't have Anthonia in her life. Bayonle's father, Michael, couldn't wear both a mother's and a father's hats, certainly not when he was more of a grandfather than a father to her due to his advanced age. Bayonle always wished Anthonia was there to teach her about those issues unique to girls. She would have loved to have Anthonia teach her about personal grooming, fashion, puberty, interpersonal relationships, even mundane things like cooking. Bayonle always wondered if her personality might have been different if she had grown up in a peaceful home with both her parents. Eventually, over time, she came to accept that she would never know.

Bayonle experienced abandonment and low self-esteem growing up. She lacked social skills, which she believed her mother could have instilled in her. She didn't have what other girls her age had: nice clothes and accessories and such, things a mother would look after in an ideal situation. Moreover, there was no connection whatsoever between her and Anthonia. This ended up affecting her relationship with her peers. She often felt they could not understand what it felt like to be in her shoes. There was always a hole inside her, one she kept trying to fill as we'll see later in the book.

5

Bayonle's Weaknesses and Insecurities

No one is perfect. Even the most confident people have insecurities. At some point in our lives, we may feel we lack something. That is reality. We must try to live as per our capability. — Anil Sinha

Every year, thousands of couples end their marriages as a last resort. The aftermath of divorce can be traumatic for the children involved. Every child deserves to be nurtured by two parents in a healthy environment. Unfortunately, this is not always the case.

So many things could go wrong when a child must be raised by people other than their parents. This was Bayonle's experience as a child from a broken home. That's not to say things can't go wrong when both parents raise their children. Parents may do everything right, yet the child still chooses the wrong path in life. There are great foster parents, adoptive parents, and guardians in the world. Some of these people would do anything to comfort the children in their care. God bless their hearts!

Studies have shown that the first two years after a divorce are the most challenging for children.[12] Bayonle is a more

12 Rappaport, S.R., "Deconstructing the Impact of Divorce on

rare breed though; her parents' issues lasted throughout her childhood up to her teenage years and into early adulthood. Parental separation or divorce has negative and long-term effects on children's behaviour, psychological well-being, and academic performance.[13] All these would later become Bayonle's struggles. Many straight "A" students and well-behaved kids become a shadow of themselves after their parents' divorce. Some just can't cope no matter how much help and resources they are given. In Bayonle's case, she didn't have the opportunity to experience her parents living together. They parted ways when she was still in diapers.

Most divorced parents have custody arrangements; some have shared custody, or one parent may have full custody of the children while the other parent has visitation privileges. This wasn't the case with Bayonle. From the time when she moved in with her maternal grandma to when she went to live with her father, her mother wasn't in the picture. And that was most of her childhood. There were no custody arrangements whatsoever. Bayonle still believes if there was some form of shared custody in her case, she might not have developed some of the behavioural, social, and psychological challenges she experienced throughout her childhood and early adulthood. Her situation left her feeling totally abandoned by her mother. Does this resonate with you?

The only way Bayonle knew how to play with other kids was in a sexual manner. In her elementary-school days, she would touch her peers inappropriately and teach younger kids around her to do the same. Something in her told her it must be wrong, but she didn't know how else to play. She just didn't

---

Children," *Family Law Quarterly*, 47, no. 3 (2013): 353-377.

13 Elliott, B. J., and M. P. Richards. "Effects of parental divorce on children." *Archives of Disease in Childhood*, 66, no. 8 (1991): 915.

know any better!

She just thought it was normal until one afternoon.

During the school break, Bayonle was asked to babysit her neighbour's kids. She was eleven at the time; the kids were five and seven years old. They were "playing" as she had instructed them to "play" when another neighbour, Mrs. Ade, came home and saw what the kids were doing in the hallway. She yelled at the top of her voice. She dispersed the kids and had "the talk" with Bayonle. Mrs. Ade said that what Bayonle had asked the kids to do was wrong and warned her never to do it again. That was the last Bayonle ever heard about it. She never did know if Mrs. Ade had told the children's parents anything or if maybe she just decided to keep an eye on Bayonle herself.

That day, Bayonle realized her way of "playing" was the dirt and the dross in her coming to light. Yet no matter how thick darkness may be, when light comes, darkness disappears. So, looking back thirty-five years later, Bayonle feels it was mercy that found her that day. It was light dispersing the darkness. Much more damage would have eventually been done if she hadn't gotten caught that early in life. However, at the time, her insecurity, fear, and shame stared her in the face.

Bayonle felt defeated and confused after the incident. She retreated to her shell for a long time. She was ashamed of herself and cried whenever she was alone, wondering why those boys that had abused her had been put in her path. Her retreat affected her socially. She lost confidence in herself. Her fear was she might mess up again if she tried to befriend her peers. Does this resonate with you?

Holidays were hard for Bayonle, especially when her two older sisters moved to another state. Unfortunately, at just twelve, that meant she was responsible for taking care of the house. As young as she was, she did everything in the house: shopping, cooking, cleaning, and the laundry. She went to school Monday to Friday. She came home to prepare supper. On Saturdays, she would go grocery shopping, do the cooking, cleaning, and the laundry. The heavyweight of adult responsibilities rested on her shoulders. She didn't have the opportunity to be a child. When other kids would talk about how they spent their weekend, doing fun stuff, watching television, and going on playdates, Bayonle couldn't say the same. Again, this affected her socially; she felt left out and isolated.

Eventually, her peers stopped inviting her to functions. This was partly because they knew she didn't have clothes to wear for the occasion and partly because her social skills weren't on par with her peers. All these just created more insecurity in Bayonle. She became overly quiet.

With longing, she admired the other kids' nice clothes at Easter and Christmas while going without herself. With yearning, she watched them eat the special dishes their mothers prepared, like jollof rice and fried rice with chicken and *dodo oniyeri* (fried ripe plantains with tomatoes, peppers, and eggs). She didn't have a mother or older siblings that could make any of those delicacies. There was no one to teach her either.

Michael and Bayonle didn't go visiting during Easter or Christmas, and no one visited them either. Bayonle always thought that if there had been a good father-child relationship between Michael and his children, things would have been different. Other children would visit their extended families during the holidays, but not Bayonle. Holidays are a special time when families can catch up on what's going on in one another's world, share meals, bond with grandchildren, and so on. Unfortunately, Bayonle didn't experience any of that. To Bayonle, the holidays were like any other time of the year except that she got to make chicken on Christmas. Yes, they only got to eat chicken once a year. It was another side effect of their poverty. Despite Michael's hard work even in his old age, they still couldn't make ends meet.

In her article, "Holiday Time for Children of Divorce," Risa Garon highlights some of the challenges children of divorced parents encounter during holiday seasons. Perhaps quite logically, children want to experience what they see on television and the internet during the holiday season, such as the traditional opening of presents, big dinners, and going to the movies. At the same time, they feel alone. They also feel intimidated by their parents' new significant others.[14]

Bayonle didn't have a television at home growing up because they couldn't afford one. However, she would go to her neighbours' rooms to watch television, so she did have some grasp of what holidays were like for "normal" families. On the upside, going to the neighbour's place to watch television was much like going to the cinema for her. Sometimes though, she had to sneak out to watch television at the neighbours' place. Michael regarded watching television as a distraction, and he didn't want anything to affect Bayonle's education negatively. At least, that's what he said.

Inferiority complex was another demon that tormented Bayonle. As per a 2016 study, "Inferiority complex refers to feeling inferior and generating shame, shyness, frustration, fear, and other complex emotions when people evaluate themselves."[15] Studies have linked inferiority complex in

14 Garon, Risa, "Holiday Time for Children of Divorce," *Huffpost*. Updated December 18, 2016, https://www.huffpost.com/entry/holi-day-time-for-children_b_8832504

15 Kong, Xiangna, and Wang, Shengyang, "The Relationship between Interparental Conflict Perception and Inferiority Complex of Junior School Students," In *Proceedings of the 2016 International Conference*

children to parental-conflict perception. Michael never had anything good to say about Anthonia and vice versa, so Bayonle grew up to know her parents as each other's worst enemy. This explains Bayonle's lack of self-confidence and her feeling of "I'm not good enough." She often thought if her foundation had been stronger, more stable, she could have been a better version of herself.

At the same time, low self-esteem inundated Bayonle. She was emotionally unstable. Michael may not have abused her physically like he did her older siblings, but the tone with which he corrected her made her feel less than her peers. This affected her confidence as a young girl. Whenever she was asked to join a group or take part in an activity in school or church, she often felt incompetent. She had no present father or mother to cheer her up or motivate her to discover her talents and develop them. She felt no one was there to support her and she was also always afraid of trying new things, public speaking, and participating in sports. She had all the physical features of an athlete, but psychologically, she couldn't handle it. For example, a lady in her church said she should join the choir because she had a good voice, so Bayonle gave it a try. Then when she was in middle school, she was asked to lead a song during a special church event. As much as she tried, she couldn't project her voice when the day finally came despite weeks of rehearsals. One of the leaders had to take the microphone from her to save the day. She was so embarrassed. It took her a long time to recover from the mortification. Given Bayole's real-life experiences, there might be something to all the studies that say inferiority complex and low self-esteem stem directly from parental divorce.

---

on Advances in Management, Arts and Humanities Science, Taiwan-Taichung, December 10–11, 2016, 519 522, Atlantis Press, 2016, Retrieved February 12, 2022, from https://www.atlantis-press.com/proceedings/amahs-16/25865871

6

Prevention: Avoid Future Troubles

When people appear to be something other than good and decent, it is only because they are reacting to stress, pain, or the deprivation of basic human needs such as security, love, and self-esteem.
— Abraham Maslow[16]

To prevent means "*to keep from happening or existing*" according to the Merriam-Webster Dictionary.[17]

Prevention of future troubles for your children starts before marriage. One of the greatest decisions people make in life is that of who to marry. The traditional marriage vow ends with, "Till death do us part." This vow implies the ideal marriage is a journey of no return and that death is the only thing that should end a marriage. In light of this, it's imperative that people be cautious while dating so they don't miss the warning signs of a less than ideal match. All red flags should be looked at critically. If there's any signal of impending danger or trouble, one must disengage from the relationship. Singles, *look before you leap*!

16 Cherry, Kendra, "Abraham Maslow Quotes about Psychology," *ThoughtCo*, Updated February 24, 2019, Abraham Maslow Quotes About Psychology (thoughtco.com)

17 "Prevent," Merriam-Webster Dictionary, Retrieved May 24, 2022 from https://www.merriam-webster.com/dictionary/prevent

Bayonle still believes that the trauma Anthonia and Michael experienced growing up affected their marriage. Anthonia and Michael were both abused in their childhood and early adulthood. There is no record that either sought therapy, nor did they ever say they did. As far as Bayonle is concerned, her parents carried all their junk into their marriage, and they were both drowned by it. They could not save the ship of their marriage from wrecking. Michael carried both the pain of his childhood abuse and the trauma of losing two children to his first wife—who claimed Michael was impotent—and Anthonia carried the pain of literally being disengaged from her first love by her relatives. She was probably still grieving the loss of Mr. Ade, the father of her first child when the community elders married her to Michael. And all this pain was more than enough to ruin their marriage before it even began.

Perhaps, if Michael and Anthonia had gone for therapy for their traumas before their marriage, they could have had a happily ever after. Another option Bayonle thought might have increased the odds of a successful marriage for Michael and Anthonia is separation, to allow each party freedom to work on themselves. They could always have come back together once they were ready to give their marriage another chance. Marriage is neither a Band-Aid nor a therapy in and of itself for two broken people. Bayonle always sensed—even as a young child—that Michael's abusive way of disciplining his children, his anger, and his controlling attitude toward Anthonia were a result of his past disappointment and betrayal from the people he loved.

Consequently, Bayonle felt totally abandoned by her mother growing up. Anthonia wasn't in the picture; she gave Bayonle over to others when she was just a toddler. This just goes to show how important it is for separated or divorced parents to have a well-structured coparenting arrangement. To this day, Bayonle is positive that if an arrangement like that had been in place, she would have had a different, and possibly decent, childhood. And that would have equalled an ounce of prevention.

***

As she got older, Bayonle was eager to break the chain of poverty in her family so she could prevent a similar life for future generations of her family. The first thing she focused on was education. Education is one key way poverty can be averted. And she knew this. She fought tooth and nail to get a good education, and it paid off in the end. Not everyone gets to go to college; many people want to go but can't afford it. University and college may be too expensive—and they may not interest you—but there are private and public institutions in every nation around the world where people can learn trades. The trades are admirable and authentic. They're specialized knowledge you can learn hands-on and use to improve your life and future. Some countries have informal training centres where people can learn plumbing, catering, carpentry, sewing, farming, and more. Look at the options and the support available in your community. You can acquire the knowledge you need to escape from poverty by attending either formal or informal educational institutions. Explore the resources available to you in your area such as scholarships and education grants. You might need to combine working part-time with schooling, but it's a short-term sacrifice for long-term gain.

One major barrier to gaining an education is not knowing

which career path to take. Career counsellors are available everywhere. The name may be different in your country. Some countries call them guidance counsellors, career coaches, or career-guidance therapists. Talk to a counsellor; they will help you discover your passion and how to develop it, and in many places, you can find one for free.

***

On another note, there is a second crisis you need to ensure prevention of substance abuse. There are young adults, who are supposed to be the leaders of tomorrow, living without a purpose or a clear direction for their lives. Some have drug-induced mental illness. Some have suffered irreversible brain damage due to drug misuse in their formative years.

The long-term effects of substance abuse are damaging to every bodily system. For example, cocaine use causes fatigue, persistent cough, difficulty breathing, pulmonary infection, nosebleeds, death of nasal linings and sinuses, metabolism alteration, eating disorders, malnutrition, bowel ischemia, high blood pressure, heart disease, heart attack, loss of brain volume, permanent destruction of brain cells, seizures, hallucination, paranoia, and aging. [18]

The side effects listed above can make illicit drug users unable to function effectively in society. If they have children, their children may suffer neglect, abandonment, and abuse. Children tend to mirror their parents and other adults in their lives. Children can then start to experiment with illicit drugs

---

18 Mosel, Stacy, "Brain Damage from Drugs & Alcohol (Are Effects Reversible?)," *American Addiction Centers*, Edited by Amelia Sharp, Updated May 202, 2022, https://americanaddictioncenters.org/alcoholism-treatment/brain-damage

early in life; hence the cycle continues from generation to generation. Does this resonate with you? The best thing you can do for you, for your children, or for your future children, is to get help. If you already have children, they will benefit from seeing you be strong enough to get help. They will admire you for loving them enough to do so. That is what can keep them from following the same destructive path. Prevention is the best medicine!

Before we move on, as a survivor of parental divorce, childhood sexual abuse, and poverty, I want to address parents and parents-to-be. Your responsibility is to provide for the people you bring into the world. These children did not choose their parents; you chose to have them. It's quite disturbing to hear some parents call their child(ren) a mistake just because they didn't want to have them yet or weren't ready to have them yet. This is disgraceful! Guess what? No one is ever fully ready. So take responsibility for your actions when it happens to you. Take charge of the change in your life's direction. When two people become intimate sexually, they should not be surprised when pregnancy occurs. It's like a chemist who combined sodium and chlorine and when the results appeared said, "Oh, I didn't want it to be salt!" What you make is what you'll get.

A child's foundation is integral. Children do not have control over their origin. It lies solely on the parents. What foundation did you build for your children? The formative years from infancy to age eight are crucial in a child's life. During these years, children learn more quickly than at any other stage of their lives. They develop intellectually, physically, emotionally, and socially. Their personality is formed at this stage. This is why parents need to be present and positively active in their child's life. Parents greatly determine the course of a child's life.

I want to suggest that parents prepare very well before they bring innocent children into the world. Just as one prepares for a career by obtaining formal or informal education, one should do the same when it comes to raising children. There are valuable resources available about intentional parenting. There are parental classes nowadays that were not available to Bayonle's parents fifty years ago. Please acquire all the knowledge you can before and during pregnancy. Parenting is a life journey, and one can't afford to mess it up. This too is an ounce of prevention.

***

Those who were terribly wounded in their childhood didn't experience a normal life growing up. Their normal is likely not the same as their peers. Some may even create their own fantasy world. Their innate longing to be loved and protected could lead them into damaging situations. This is why predators target them. Bayonle can relate to this; after all, that's how she grew up.

Your future lies in your own hands once you're old enough to make decisions on your own, and more so when you become an adult. You can say "enough is enough," "I want to change my narrative," 'I want to rebrand my life," and "I'm not a child anymore, so it's high time I stood up for myself and redefined my future." You're not a loser! You can achieve anything you want with perseverance. And you can let your healing journey begin today. How you begin your healing is totally up to you and what you want to focus on. There are experienced therapists you can work with. The power is in your hands!

Oftentimes we don't know the power embedded in us or we misuse or misdirect the power. Taking the first step is the most difficult task in the healing process for childhood sexual abuse victims. Another challenge is fear: fear of what people will say or how people will react to their story has kept some survivors muted for so long. Bayonle experienced this fear. But even though the damage has been done, repair is possible. Seek help! Use the power of your voice by telling someone that can listen and help. Go for counselling. Look for resources available to you locally. Some countries have helplines for victims of abuse. Pick up the phone; call that number. It's important to talk to people that are trained so you avoid being retraumatized. The goal of therapy is to provide safety, choice, and control to victims. People that are not trained may not know how to approach your situation or know the right questions to ask.

If you have children or you planned to have children in the future, I suggest you watch out for them. Even as you take care of you, do all you can to protect your children from predators. Start by developing a good relationship with them such that they can trust you enough to share anything with you. As we saw in Pat's story in the preface of this book, parent-child relationships shouldn't be servant-master relationships. In this type of relationship, the children don't feel loved and aren't able to share their struggles with their parents. On the other hand, parents should not become passive and turn a blind eye when their children need to be corrected. Your love for your children will propel you to discipline them with love.

Sex education too is important; children need to know about their body parts when they're old enough to learn, generally between eighteen months and three years. They need to know that their body belongs to them, and they need to know the proper names for their private parts: genitals (penis, vagina). They need to know no one can touch their private parts except those providing the necessary care at the necessary time, such as parents and health-care providers during such processes as exams and bathing. Children also need to know they can't touch other people's private parts. This education must continue as they grow older, from school age (5-8 years old) through to preteens (9-12 years old) and the teenage years.[19] [20]

19 SickKids Staff, "Sexuality: what children should learn and why," *SickKids*, Retrieved May 23, 2022, from https://www.aboutkidshealth.ca/Article?contentid=716&language=English#:~:text=Pre%2Dteens%3A%20Nine%20to%2012,sexually%20transmitted%20infections%20(STIs)

20 Schmidt, Courtney, "How and why to talk to your kids about their private parts," *Orlando Health, Arnold Palmer Hospital for Children*, March 29, 2018, https://www.arnoldpalmerhospital.com/content-hub/how-and-why-to-talk-to-your-kids-about-their-private-parts

PART 2

PROTECTION

7

Bayonle's Elementary School Life

Despite Bayonle's mommy issues and the abuse that became her norm, she was brilliant in school. She became a favourite student of some of the teachers. In those days in Nigeria, if your peers heard that your teacher had invited you to their house, they would be jealous.

The first time Miss Adigun invited Bayonle to her house, Bayonle's jaw dropped. She closed her eyes and jumped, then twirled around. Miss Adigun just stood there speechless. After a few seconds, she finally asked, "So Bayonle, would you come to my place after school on Friday?" Bayonle's eyes got teary and her face warmed as she responded, "Yes, yes, Ma." Bayonle wished Miss Adigun would adopt her. Subconsciously, and perhaps even consciously, she wanted a female role model, someone she could talk to and call Mom. She had always missed having her mother in her life. When her peers talked about their parents, especially their mothers, Bayonle had nothing to say. Even at home, she was the only child in the building without a mother. She thought her life would be changed forever if Miss Adigun could fill the vacuum. Unfortunately, her wish didn't see the light of day, though Bayonle did go to Miss Adigun's house a few times. She helped Miss Adigun with chores and watched TV with her, while Miss Adigun gave her food and snacks. Those were wonderful times.

***

Adeola was one of Bayonle's friends. She liked everything about Adeola. Her skin was flawless. She was neat and tidy. She came to school in her pretty, well-ironed, green school uniform. In contrast, Bayonle would always have to mend her school uniform a few times before her father could afford to get her a new one. Moreover, she had to use nails or a needle and thread to mend her torn sandals numerous times. Poverty dealt with her mercilessly. This often made her question her future. Would it be bright or bleak?

Adeola and her twin brother, Adeolu, would always bring tantalizing food to school for lunch. One day they might have yam and scrambled eggs or a simple bread and butter sandwich, and some days they might have white rice with fish stew or jollof rice or fried rice with chicken. These foods were not on the menu at Bayonle's house. They only ate chicken once a year during Christmas.

Bayonle always wondered why Adeola and Adeolu appeared so polished compared to their peers. Eventually, she determined it was because the twins' mom was a registered nurse. For Bayonle, this explained why they were always neat and ate good, nutritious food. As she had with her teacher, Bayonle wished Adeola's mom was her mom and often daydreamed about her future children. She wanted them to be well fed, nourished, attractive, and neat like the twins.

Malnutrition was endemic among children during Bayonle's childhood. Many children were hospitalized due to *kwashiorkor* (severe protein malnutrition) and *marasmus* (life-threatening, nutrition-deficiency disorder). In a bid to control malnutrition, the government initiated programs to create awareness about locally available and affordable nutritious foods. One of such foods was soybeans. The government created an enormous campaign to explain different ways of processing soybeans at home: soy milk, tofu, porridge, even soup. Government staff would go to schools, clinics, markets, and places of worship to educate people on how to use soybeans in different forms. Because of its nutritional value, soybeans became a food that people added to every meal. Mothers would add soy flour to baking and even to infant-weaning diets.

The government also made it mandatory for students to have lunch in school. Elementary students had to buy food from food vendors that the government mandated had to be at an affordable price. Every morning all the students would place their labelled food containers at the front of the classroom. Then the food vendors would pick them up and return them before lunch break with food.

Bayonle's favourite food was bean porridge. A good dish of bean porridge is savoury. Each bite is warm, hearty, and delicious. Bayonle could still eat bean porridge three times a day. Others must have felt the same because some developed a habit of putting *gari* (cassava flakes) in their containers, so the food vendor would serve the beans on top. Some would even wet their *gari* the night before so it would expand.

Bayonle got curious. She wanted more from her *gari*, so she decided to experiment one day. She moistened her *gari* on a Friday afternoon with the hope that it would triple or quadruple by Monday. She was disappointed by the result when she opened her bowl and saw green *gari* instead. It had become mouldy in those sixty hours due to the heat. Lesson learned!

8

Run! Run!! Run!!!

Like most young kids, Bayonle had a crush on a boy in her class. One day, she decided she would write him a letter. So, she did. However, she inadvertently left the letter in Michael's chair in the balcony. When Michael found the letter as he removed the cushion, he read it. Bayonle could not even deny that she had written it as she had signed her name! Moreover, he could recognize her writing in the dark. Her defence was that they were learning letter writing in school, and the teacher asked students to practice at home. Somehow, she got away with it. Perhaps five years earlier, Michael would have beaten her black and blue as he had her older siblings. But aging took so many things away from Michael, including the way he disciplined his children.

Michael was a tough disciplinarian. He would scold his children both verbally and with a rod. His style of discipline was extreme. His children often wished he would never return when he went on a business trip. If they were chit-chatting before he came home, they would disappear the moment they heard his voice. None would dare challenge his rage. If parents treated their children like that in present day, they could go to prison for child abuse, child neglect, and/or assault and battery. The children's fear of Michael did a lot of damage to their relationship with him.

To be fair, Michael had it rough too. His discipline style and the punishment he meted out to his children had only been passed on to him and his siblings by the generation before. According to the American Academy of Child and Adolescent Psychiatry, a child that was physically abused may grow up to think physical abuse is okay.[21] Remember, Michael was bullied and assaulted by his siblings and their friends when he was young; it was so bad that he had to leave his hometown. Moreover, his first wife divorced him and left with the children Michael believed were his. This is not an excuse for Michael's parenting and disciplining style, but rather an examination of the long-term effects of trauma on the victims.

For the most part, Bayonle couldn't fathom how her dad didn't seem to age, especially when compared to what aging tends to look like today. However, Bayonle knew three important things about Michael that may well have been responsible for Michael's ageless life. Michael didn't eat processed food, and he didn't smoke or drink alcohol during his lifetime. He even power-walked five kilometres twice a day. And on one fateful day, Bayonle would have felt Michael's physical strength if not for her shrewdness.

Bayonle ran for her dear life the day Michael would have used the rod on her. As mentioned earlier, she followed him almost everywhere. This wasn't her choice but his. They often went to see his customers. On this particular day, a customer offered them snacks, and Michael declined—as was usual. So, the customer gave Bayonle a snack, and she accepted it. In

21 American Academy of Child and Adolescent Psychiatry, "Physical Punishment," No. 105, Updated March 2018, https://www.aacap.org/AACAP/Families_and_Youth/Facts_for_Families/FFF-Guide/Physical-Punishment-105.aspx

Yoruba culture, if you're a child accompanying an adult and the adult doesn't accept food or drink from their host, that's a cue for you to also say no. As such, on their way home, Michael scolded Bayonle for accepting the snack and vowed to beat the hell out of her when they get home. So she dropped Michael's bag and ran out of the house as soon as they got home. Bayonle had seen him beat one of her older sisters numerous times; she couldn't stand it. Hence, she ran for her life. She would later find out that when Michael was younger, he would ask his children to take their clothes off before he beat them with a whip, and he would not stop until he saw blood.

Everyone, even the neighbours, helped Michael search for Bayonle. But she was desperate to escape Michael's rod, so she went back to Michael's shop, then played with some of the children in the area before she trudged back home late in the evening. Then she hid under the staircase. She could hear everyone discuss where to look for her. They walked up and down the streets, talked to other neighbours, and went to her school with flashlights as there was a power outage; she was nowhere to be found. Finally, one of the neighbours suggested they search around the house. Finally, they found her in her little haven around midnight. She screamed, "I'm a ghost! I'm a ghost! Don't come near me! Don't touch me!" That's how much she dreaded her father's lashes. In the end, he didn't beat her but warned her sternly not to accept anything from anyone unless he instructed her to do so. What a lesson that was—perhaps for both of them.

9

Bayonle's First Divine Encounter

Bayonle was raised in an orthodox church. Despite her regular church attendance, she didn't have a personal relationship with God until her midteens when she joined the Charismatic Renewal group at church. This group was known for intense prayer and deep spiritual growth. She started studying the Bible to better understand the concept of prayer, the creation, and the love of God.

Then one fall in the early nineties, another church organized a three-day camp meeting. On the second day of the crusade, the preacher made an altar call and prayed for those who want to surrender their lives to Jesus, and make him their Saviour and Lord. Seeing her need for the Redeemer and His transforming love. Bayonle surrendered her life to Jesus that evening, and an indescribable joy filled her heart. This was the beginning of a new era in her life. Goodbye to the era of lust, traumatic pain, depression, and suicidal thoughts. She felt light. Her weight had been lifted. For the first time in her short life, she had hope; there was no more darkness. Her healing had begun!

Bayonle believes that God was always there watching over her. Her life is proof that no matter what people go through in life, all will be well if you can trust God with your life. Healing journeys are different from person to person. For some, it can take months; for others, it can take years. And for most still, it can become a lifetime journey. The most important thing to take with you is that every victim needs healing. Turning to God genuinely and allowing God's Love flood one's heart and soul is the way to heal indeed – the way to experience supernatural healing, newness and wholeness that last.

10

The Arrival of a Role Model

Bayonle liked science in school. Her favourite subject was chemistry. She enjoyed going to chemistry lab and mixing chemicals to form compounds. No wonder she got an "A" in chemistry in the West African Examination Council exam. This was a mandatory final exam for grade twelve students across West Africa. She also liked Christian Religious Knowledge (CRK).

Bayonle started reading the Bible when she had to take CRK because she went to a Catholic elementary and high school. She liked reading Jesus's stories and the accounts of other Bible characters like Abraham. She and Michael went to church regularly. During school break, he would wake her up to go to morning Mass, though as much as she liked going to Mass, half the time she would pretend to go but then tiptoe back to her room. She liked her sleep!

Bayonle always looked forward to CRK class. The textbook was the Bible, which the school gave to each student. Reading the Bible became part of her routine. During school break one year, she decided to fast for three days. She had read that Jesus had fasted for forty days and forty nights, so she decided to experiment. Although she doesn't remember vividly what she specifically prayed about, she'd always wanted to know God. She desired a beautiful life, a life devoid of trauma, heartache, and poverty. She yearned for someone she could look up to, someone she could go to for advice and guidance, so she knows she kept that in her heart as she prayed.

Here's one of her pleas to God:

> Dear God,
>
> I've heard so many things about you. I'm convinced beyond a reasonable doubt that you can do all things.
> So why's my life like this?
> Where's my mother?
> Why is it that I don't have what my mates have?
> Why is my dad this strict?
> Is he really my father?
> I'm fed up with life.
> Please do something ...

***

Tayo was a young adult in one of Nigeria's colleges. Like Bayonle, Tayo also struggled financially in school. One day, she ran into Doug, a successful entrepreneur, in her first year of college when she was in dire need of money. Tayo was nineteen at the time and Doug was twenty-nine; they were from the same town. They had once been neighbours back when Tayo was six. Doug was one of the suppliers for Tayo's school. On the day they met, he had stopped by the school to deliver his quote on a project when he saw Tayo in the hallway. After that, when Doug went to Tayo's school on business, usually once a month, he would check up on Tayo each time. He would pay her tuition and buy her groceries. Initially, Tayo thought Doug was just being kind and generous. Unbeknownst to Tayo, Doug had a mission.

Toward the end of her second year in school, Doug began to act odd. He would ask her to tell him how her day and week was. He would ask for details. At first, Tayo thought Doug was only playing the role of the big brother Tayo never had. Then at the beginning of the first semester of Tayo's third year, Doug asked Tayo what she planned to do after graduation. Tayo said she would look for a job. Doug said, "No, we will get married." Tayo was shocked! So she told him that he was like a brother to her and that she couldn't marry her brother. Tayo couldn't understand what put the idea of marriage in Doug's head. She began to question whether she'd been giving Doug the wrong signals for the past year.

Doug refused to take no for answer, and he continued to pester Tayo. At one point, he started stalking her. He attempted to rape her twice when he came for his usual "visit". The second time he tried, he pinned Tayo to the wall and tore her shirt. She pushed him away and yelled for help, so Doug fled! Afterward, Tayo warned Doug never to visit her again; she threatened to call the police if she ever laid eyes on him again.

Tayo was traumatized by this incident. It took her a long time to stop blaming herself. Tayo was a Christian; she found healing in prayer and the word of God. She attended counselling sessions with her pastor, and over time, she overcame her pain.

Yinka was the breadwinner in her family of five. Her father had passed away when she was eleven. Her mother was an elementary school teacher, who took early retirement and used most of the pension to send Yinka, her first child, to college with the hope that when she graduated, she would get a good job and help send her three siblings to school. Then her mother used the other part of her pension to set up a small business to help them eat and pay rent.

Yinka graduated from university with honours and got a job right away. Unfortunately, her company suffered a great loss a year after Yinka joined them. Yinka was one of the many employees they laid off. The news was devastating for Yinka and her family. Day after day, she walked the streets of Ibadan looking for a job. She didn't want to let her family down. After six months with no job, the bills were piling up. Yinka stopped looking after herself. She didn't bathe, eat, or talk to anyone.

One day, the pastor came to Yinka's house for a welfare check as she had stopped coming to church. She blamed God for her predicament. The pastor reassured her that God loves her and that God's plans for her are good and not evil. The pastor offered her a temporary, part-time job in the church office. Then the pastor prayed with Yinka and encouraged her every day to remember that God would connect her and lead her to a good job.

Three months later, Yinka got a wonderful job that came with an official car and house in the benefits package. Yinka's first salary allowed her to pay all the outstanding debt.

Do you remember Pat from the preface? While Bayonle had mommy issues, Pat had daddy issues, and she was sexually abused as a child. She became promiscuous in her teens and between the ages of fourteen and eighteen, she had four abortions. Then God sent her a destiny helper in the form of David, one of her older siblings, after she graduated from high school. David knew about Pat's promiscuity and wanted to help her at all costs. He took Pat away from the town she had grown up in and to Benin, a bigger city, so she could have a fresh start. She even met other people in Benin who had similar childhood trauma to hers. Some surrendered their pain to the Lord in exchange for His joy. Unfortunately, Pat could not let go of her past.

Three years after Pat arrived in Benin, she eloped with James, one of her boyfriends from high school. Other men were interested in dating Pat, but she wouldn't budge because of her obsession with James. David and everyone else that Pat confided in about her childhood trauma had warned Pat to cut all ties with James. This was because James was equally abused as a child by two young adults, and he too became promiscuous. He had started sleeping with younger girls, including Pat, when he was fourteen.

Pat didn't listen to anyone's suggestions. To her, their relationship was meant to be because she had lost her virginity to James when she was thirteen. They'd been sleeping together at least thrice a week since then. Back then, Pat had been living with her aunt, Monica, who didn't see anything wrong with children of Pat's age sharing the same room with a boy. Monica had allowed James to move in with them because he was Pat's friend and they both went to the same school. James's parents too were okay with the idea.

Eventually, the consequence of their hasty marriage reared its ugly head: James and Pat were both abusive in their marriage—as predicted by David and others.

Research has shown that people who experienced sexual abuse in their childhood are susceptible to abusive relationships in their adult years.[22] Pat and James were two wounded lions who didn't tend their wounds before they married, and as a result, they became toxic to each other. James

22 Hartney, Elizabeth, "9 Reasons the Cycle of Abuse Continues," *Verywell Mind*, Updated February 16, 2022, https://www.verywellmind.com/the-cycle-of-sexual-abuse-22460

would leave Pat and the children for days and months without any communication. Eventually, he left Pat for another woman after the birth of Pat's third child. With no financial support from James, Pat was left alone to fend for their two teenage boys and their eight-year-old boy.

Day after day, year after year, Pat wished she had listened to the destiny helpers God had sent her. She imagined how her life would have been different had she embraced her destiny helpers' suggestions. Although life is tough for Pat and her boys now, she takes solace in prayer and the word of God. She's going to counselling. She's hopeful that one day, her life will turn around.

***

For Bayonle, the healing journey wasn't smooth either; it was more like a rollercoaster. She would be okay emotionally one day and fall apart the next. She needed someone to guide her in her newfound faith. She needed a mentor, someone that had the spiritual understanding of the dynamics in her life. She prayed to God for help.

The answer to her prayer came after Nigeria created Osun State in 1991. It was part of what used to be Oyo State. The government then ordered civil servants in Oyo State affiliated with Osun State by birth or marriage to move to the new Osun State. The same went for Oyo State civil servants. This would eventually work to Bayonle's advantage, reroute her path, and shape her life.

Coincidentally, one of Bayonle's half-sisters, Agnes, was married to an Osun State indigene. When the new regulations came in, Agnes was transferred from Oyo State to the city where Bayonle and Michael lived. Agnes and Bayonle had no relationship before her sister's transfer. But they later bonded so well that Bayonle started calling her "Mom." Agnes was actually old enough to be her mother given the twenty-five year age gap between them.

Bayonle was sixteen when Agnes came to live with them. Agnes took the time to watch Bayonle closely and soon discovered that she was following a dangerous path. She noticed how Bayonle interacted with boys, and an inner voice probably told her something wasn't right. Perhaps it was a mother's instinct!

So one evening, Agnes asked Bayonle to go for a walk with her. It was a memorable evening! Twilight had just dropped her curtains. The big blue sky gave way to yellow, orange, and red as they walked. The cool breeze whisked away the moisture on their skin from the heat in the house.

Bayonle was in for an experience that would turn her life around. Agnes wasn't judgemental in her approach. She just made Bayonle realize how important and indispensable she was as a girl and made her feel good about herself. She coached Bayonle to let go of her insecurities and inferiority complex. Agnes told her she could be great and that she can achieve anything she set her heart to achieve. Agnes told Bayonle she could move mountains.

As a schoolteacher and a mother to three teenage girls herself, Agnes had all the tools to advise Bayonle. These were Agnes's words:

> I see the way you interact with boys, and I wonder where you will be in the next few years. You're a teenager. I get that. Your hormones are very active. Boys and girls want to experience sex at this stage. The truth is that it's premature. You're still young, and you can't comprehend

> the true meaning of love at this time. If you sleep around and you become pregnant, the boy will probably continue with his studies while you carry the pregnancy and become a teenage mom.
>
> Face your studies squarely. Focus on you and your future. When you're successful, good men will chase after you, and by then, you'll be emotionally mature [enough] for a marital relationship.

Agnes's words of wisdom felt like someone had removed a blindfold from Bayonle's face. A girl that doesn't receive admiration and affirmation from her father *will* try to get it from any male figure willing to say the "right" words. Studies have shown that girls who have a supportive, communicative relationship with their father are less likely to become sexually active and less likely to become pregnant during their teenage years. Girls with strong relationships with their fathers are also less likely to be talked into sex. They manage stress well, and they're not overly sensitive or reactive. They attract men who are emotionally intimate and fulfilling, and they more likely have long-lasting marriages.[23]

Bayonle couldn't say she had a supportive father-daughter relationship with Michael. There were only two areas he concentrated on with her: education and church. There was no talking about sex education or how to deal with boys; her emotional needs and social needs were not tended to. Mind

23 Nielsen, Linda, "How Dads Affect Their Daughters into Adulthood," Institute for Family Studies, Updated June 3, 2014, https://ifstudies.org/blog/how-dads-affect-their-daughters-into-adulthood#:~:text=An%20emerging%20body%20of%20research,with%20their%20dads%20during%20childhood

you, Michael was in his late nineties at this point. Can one say age wasn't on his side? How could a ninety-year-old parent a teenager?

Agnes's advice broke Bayonle, and at the same time, moulded her. Bayonle couldn't believe she finally had a mother figure in her life. Agnes was her guardian angel in human form. It felt like Agnes brought a bulldozer, tractor, and a digger into Bayonle's life. Agnes's tools demolished the after taste that the pedophiles and sexual predators had left in Bayonle's mouth. The equipment plowed through her heart and removed the venom. They scraped the filthiness out of her heart and laid the good soil. Agnes began to plant positive seeds in Bayonle's life that would later become a source of healing for her wounded soul.

As this common saying says, "*A friend in need is a friend indeed,*" Agnes became a "mother indeed" to Bayonle. She planted love, patience, forgiveness, peace, kindness, resilience, joy, and self-discipline in her.

The connection between Agnes and Bayonle wasn't hard to believe. Agnes was abused physically and emotionally just like Michael's other children. She knew how poverty could ruin a child's life. One story Agnes told Bayonle happened when Agnes got her first salary as a teacher. She bought all kinds of food she had never eaten growing up. And for supper that night, she made rice and beef stew. For seasoning, Agnes used ten teaspoons of curry, thyme, and white pepper to cook two pounds of beef. Her thought was the more seasoning she added, the tastier her beef would be. Unfortunately, it didn't work that way; the stew wasn't edible. She later learned from people who knew how to properly use these seasonings that she'd never been exposed to.

As high-school graduation drew near, Bayonle became

apprehensive. She thought about what she would do on that day; maybe she would not attend the school graduation. The more she thought about what to do, the more the ideas deserted her. Bayonle's main concern was that she had nothing to wear to her graduation ceremony. She thought Agnes had already gone above and beyond for her, so she didn't want to put the burden of a grad dress on her shoulders.

Then Bayonle had a thought: Anthonia, her birth mother. Well, the problem with that was that Bayonle had no relationship with Anthonia. They had never even spoken. Her only memory of Anthonia was Bayonle's near-death experience when she was around five.

Anthonia and her new husband had a shop close to the main road. It was a fairly busy street. Little Bayonle had wanted to cross the road while a cab was approaching. When he saw Bayonle, the cab driver swerved to avoid hitting her. There had been a loud noise and everyone around her had screamed. Then the driver slammed on the brakes.

"Bayonle! Bayonle! Eh! Eh! I'm in trouble oh!" Anthonia had yelled. All the bystanders had wanted to tear the cab driver to pieces. He had knelt then and looked under the car … and there was little Bayonle, lying on her tummy and looking like a shy kitten. Boy, had she been scared! Anthonia had sobbed when she finally held Bayonle in her arms. Thankfully, little Bayonle sustained no injuries!

At seventeen and in her final year in high school, she still couldn't fathom how she ended up under the car instead of being hit. *Truly, children have guardian angels*, she thought regularly.

When Bayonle could not think of what else to do about her grad dress, she summoned her courage and wrote a long letter to Anthonia. It described how her absence in Bayonle's life had negatively impacted her.

Dear Mother,
I hope this letter meets you well! How's your husband? How're my siblings? How's your business going?

I miss you. I miss having a female figure in my life. Going through puberty without you was devastating for me to say the least. No one to show me girl stuff. No one prepared me for the changes I experienced in my body. I didn't wear a bra until I was 15. I ran to my friend's place when I had my first period. I didn't know what to do. I used pieces of clothes as menstrual pads. I had accidents so many times. A lot of things would have been different for me if only you had been here. I can't blame you really. You have to do what is best for you.

My father is trying his best, but it's not the same as having an adult female around. Sister Agnes is staying with us Monday to Friday. She moved in with us shortly after the creation of Osun State. She's been my rock! She has taught me a lot of things. She helps me define my relationship with boys. My cooking skill is better because of her. I can make *egusi* soup the right way now. And lest I forget, she bought me a Bible. Please thank her when you see her.

The purpose of writing you this letter is about my high-school graduation. As you already know, the dress code is white attire. I don't have a white dress and no accessories. Could you please make me a beautiful grad dress? I would also like a pair of lilac shoes and a bag to match. I wear size 10 shoes. You know I've never asked you for anything all my life.

Thank you in anticipation of your favourable response!

Your daughter,
Bayonle

Bayonle's greatest need then was a grad dress, and she wasn't shy about it in her letter to Anthonia. She had never had the privilege of a variety of clothes as her peers growing up. This was partly because of poverty and partly because Michael would only buy clothes for her once a year. Most of the time, they were not clothes she wanted to wear. She couldn't blame him. He was in his nineties at the time, and though he was physically fit and would still go to his shop Monday to Saturday, he didn't know what was in style or in fashion. For reasons known only to him, he wouldn't give Bayonle money to go shopping for herself.

Fortunately, Agnes found Bayonle's letter to Anthonia and read it. Agnes advised Bayonle not to send the letter and promised that she would take care of Bayonle's grad wardrobe. And Agnes did, oh so well! Agnes had known Anthonia might not be able to afford the type of dress Bayonle wanted, partly because Anthonia and her husband, Tunde, were equally struggling to make ends meet. So even though as far as Bayonle could recall, throughout her school years, Anthonia hadn't bought her any clothes, not even a pair of underwear, Anthonia and Tunde were not in good shape financially or emotionally either. They'd had seven children by the time Bayonle was in grade twelve. Tragically, three had died. Their twins had died at birth and a half-sister, Yomi, had died of malaria fever when she was a toddler. The losses were traumatic for them. Agnes looked at the whole situation from an adult point of view and knew asking Anthonia for a grad dress should be out of the question.

But thanks to Agnes, Bayonle's morale was boosted during her high-school graduation. For the first time, she could walk side by side with her peers without feeling inferior. Agnes had gotten her a white dress with lilac shoes and a matching purse. Bayonle finally felt confident as she congregated with her classmates. She would never forget Agnes's influence in her life. Agnes would later become an important pillar in Bayonle's support system throughout her nursing career.

Every lonely, damaged, and traumatized child needs an angel like Agnes in their life. I pray for every suffering child out there that your angel will locate you and rescue you.

11

Marriage? That's a No-Go Zone

Truth be told, it was difficult for Bayonle to even think of having a relationship with Anthonia. It was hard for her to forgive both her parents. She struggled a lot with this over the course of her life. She recounted the ordeal of her childhood regularly, remembering how the adults that were supposed to protect her had let her down. It was like everywhere she went, there was someone who would attempt to take advantage of her innocence and vulnerability.

In Bayonle's high-school days, one of the teachers asked her out. Are you kidding me, Mr. Teacher? She was only sixteen. He didn't beat around the bush in his approach either; he just blurted it out: "Bayonle, I want you to be my girlfriend." This was a married man with two children. Bayonle had toughened up and smartened up by then. She ignored him and asked herself, "What does a married man want with an innocent young adult? Why?" Then it happened again. When she was eighteen, a priest asked her out when she was in midwifery school. And then she asked herself, "Why are these men all the same? Why does a priest who took an oath of celibacy want to sleep with me?" She concluded that the male authority figures around her were out to ruin her life.

***

Bayonle remembers one set of neighbours in particular, Mr. and Mrs. Cook, from when she was in elementary school. They were the firsthand personification of regular physical and emotional abuse. Mr. Cook would beat his wife up for no reason, yet all the neighbours knew of Mr. Cook's infidelity. He often sent the neighbour's children on errands to his numerous girlfriends. As young as Bayonle was, she wished she could help Mrs. Cook.

The most horrifying episode was when Mrs. Cook was pregnant with their last child, which made Bayonle vowed she would never get married. Mr. and Mrs. Cook were elementary school teachers. Mrs. Cook's school was close to the house, while Mr. Cook's school was about a thirty-minute drive. Mrs. Cook always got home first, and she prepared fish stew and okra soup for supper. On that fateful day, she was in the process of making *amala* (cassava flour meal) when Mr. Cook arrived. He became enraged because the *amala* wasn't ready before his arrival. The pots went flying as he turned the kitchen upside down. All the food Mrs. Cook had prepared was poured on the floor. Then he poured the cassava flour everywhere. Mrs. Cook yelled, "*Were, were*!" ("Mad man, mad man!"). Mr. Cook yelled back, "I'll show you madness today!" Then he slapped her and began to punch her. The neighbours ran to the scene and rescued her. The physical abuse and the emotional rollercoaster she watched Mrs. Cook suffer was too much for Bayonle to bear. From then on, she never wanted anyone to talk to her about marriage. To her, marriage was like sending someone to death row.

***

Amina watched her father, Chief Haruna, a wealthy entrepreneur, chase everything in a skirt when she was a child. Everyone knew about Chief Haruna's infidelity except his wife. Chief Haruna would regularly go on vacation abroad in the company of one of his numerous girlfriends. There were times he would not come home for weeks. Chief Haruna provided everything his family could need, but he was absent emotionally—and physically. His children told him many times that money could never take his place, even though he provided for them. They went to the best schools and ate the best food, but their father's escapades with women became traumatic for them, and especially for Amina, his first child.

Amina became financially buoyant like her father. However, she grew up to dislike men with a passion, and at thirty-five, she's still single despite many suitors asking for her hand in marriage. She blamed Chief Haruna for her lack of interest in marriage. She just couldn't trust men and would rather remain single all her life than marry a man that would later cheat on her. To her, all men are the same. Does this resonate with you?

12

Destiny Helpers

People always come into your life for a reason, a season, or a lifetime. When you figure out which it is, you know exactly what to do.[24] — *Brian A Chalker*

Bayonle liked going to school. One of her dreams was to be well read, have a broad perspective, and help people. She wanted to be a university professor. She believed that with education, she would transition from poverty to wealth. She didn't want her children and the next generation to experience what she had experienced. How could she achieve this goal when she could hardly feed herself though?

When she was about to graduate from high school, Agnes asked Bayonle if she would like to study nursing and that she would obtain the form for her. Without hesitation, Bayonle jumped at the offer. She had seen a few families where the woman of the house was a nurse, and she liked how healthy their children were and how well-groomed and well-behaved they were. Bayonle wanted to give her children that. Fortuitously, Agnes would continue to support her later in her

24 Motivation Posters, "A Reason A Season and A Lifetime," Retrieved from https://motivationposters.com/index.php?route=product/product&product_id=367

college days.

Bayonle was thrilled when she was accepted into the Oluyoro School of Midwifery Ibadan. Her dream of becoming a nurse like the mother of the twins in her elementary school was gradually coming true. She had been looking forward to the day when she could say, "School, here I come!" Finally, that day came in March 1994.

A few days before she left home for school, Michael called her over. With his hands crossed on his belly, he cleared his throat. "Your teachers in elementary school and high school always told me to watch out for you and make sure you go to college because you have the brain for education. You know I'm very old, I have no money, and I don't have anything I could pawn to pay your tuition." He threw his arms open wide and continued. "You know if I had sellable properties, I would sell them to send you to school." This was one of the best conversations Michael had ever had with Bayonle; She had never seen him like this before, his eyebrows drawn inward, his eyes teary. "I know God will make a way for you. Remember, daughter, who you are."

She tried to look into the future at that, but she couldn't see anything. It was blank! "Thank you, *Baba* (Father)," was all she could say. Deep within her, Bayonle knew that Michael would have provided for her education if he'd had the means. He wanted her to be well-educated, but unfortunately, he just couldn't afford it.

After her high-school graduation, Agnes advised Bayonle to get a job not only so she wouldn't become idle and bored, but also so she could make some money for college. Fortunately for her, there was a vacancy in one of the pharmacies close to their house, only about a ten-minute walk away. She applied and was hired immediately. Bayonle worked in this shop for a few months but later got a better job with increased pay at a photocopy centre. She was able to save some money in the months before college, some of which she used to prepare for school by buying some of the required school supplies and clothes.

Finally, after months of anticipation, she found herself at school. However, she had to stay in the midwifery school's hostel, where each dormitory had six spring beds. Each bed had a ceiling-high wardrobe beside it. But while the school provided a spring bed, wardrobe, and curtains; each student had to bring their own mattress. When it was time for Bayonle to go to school, neither she nor her father could afford to buy a mattress for her. They also couldn't afford half the items on the school's supply list. Out of the twenty-one students in her class, she was the only one that slept on a spring bed with no mattress. Bayonle arrived at the dormitory with a duffel bag, a plastic bag, and a mat, plus a few clothes, a mosquito net, cassava flakes, peanuts, and sugar.

Every week, she would watch her classmates go home on Fridays and come back to the hostel on Sunday with bags of groceries and supplies. Those who didn't go home enjoyed family visits on Saturday, and of course, their families brought them food and supplies. More than anything, Bayonle wished she came from a family that could shower her with everything she ever wanted, but mostly food, love, and a sense of belonging. At night when she tried to fall asleep, she would dream about her future family. Her children would go to private school. They would have an active, loving, and super father. They would have good food to eat, and she would protect them from predators.

Right from her elementary school days, Bayonle was always the last student to pay her school fees. Many nights, she went to bed with an empty stomach and no hope of having food to eat the following day. Her escape from hunger was the "accidental vegetables" on the school lawn. In the rainy season, Bayonle survived on waterleaf (ceylon spinach) she plucked from the school grounds. In Nigeria, the rainy season is between March and August. It's characterized by periods of moderate to heavy rain and the harvest of seasonal crops like fresh corn. June is the peak for accidental vegetables in Oyo State. Bayonle called them accidental vegetables as no one planted them; they just grew on their own. She thought perhaps people transported the seeds on the soles of their shoes.

During that bountiful season, Bayonle would cook waterleaf with ground pepper, a few slices of onions, salt, palm oil, and *maggi* seasoning. No meat, no fish. She would eat the soup with *eba*, which is hot water and cassava flakes. This would sometimes be the only meal she would eat that day. Other days, her "poverty meal" was a *gari* concoction. She would moisten *gari* with water, pour it in a pot, add pepper, a pinch of salt, and oil, and cook it on low heat for a few minutes. And these meals she was grateful to have.

Now Nigerian culture encourages the older siblings to raise the younger ones, including financially for poor families. It doesn't work that way for wealthy families as those parents can support their children. But as for Bayonle, she needed all the support she could get from her older siblings. Luckily, a few of her half-siblings were old enough to be her parents, so this worked well for her.

Who are destiny helpers?

Destiny helpers are people who come to one's life in a time of need. Some will show up for just one reason, and then the relationship ends. For example, if an elderly person falls on the ice on a cold winter day and can't get up due to a fractured hip, and a passerby finds them and calls an ambulance but never follows up with the victim, then, the passerby was there at the right time for a reason.

Other times, destiny helpers show up for a season. They could be in one's life for a few weeks, months, or years to complete a project or fulfill a purpose. And once the purpose is accomplished, the relationship ends. Earlier in the book, Agnes came into Bayonle's life when her life was about to take a turn for the worse. Her half-sister helped her recover the self-esteem that was long lost and gave her good advice about life issues. One could say Agnes came into Bayonle's life for a season. An example of lifetime helpers are spouses who do not separate or divorce and have a solid, supportive relationship.

To begin with, Agnes and her family fortuitously lived in Ibadan when Bayonle was attending the midwifery and nursing schools. While Bayonle happily reconnected with her before the end of the first semester, she didn't want to become a burden to her half-sister as she had her own family to take care of. But once in a while, Bayonle would go to Agnes's house for the weekend. They made her feel at home and treated her like an immediate member of the family. Her meals were guaranteed on those weekends and Agnes would give her some groceries on Sunday evening when it was time for Bayonle to go back to school. Most importantly though, she often got "maintenance" doses of Agnes's therapeutic advice.

Sadly, Bayonle did not have a relationship with most of her older siblings before the end of her first year in college. But college changed all that. It opened up her world and gave her the opportunity to get to know them. Take Mide, for example, Bayonle's maternal half-brother. He was the first to step up in her life at a time when she had no one to turn to for financial help. Mide had just graduated from the university and had landed a job in one of the universities in Ondo State. During one school break, she was invited to visit Mide and his family. After a long discussion about her struggles and lack of financial aid, Mide offered to help. He paid Bayonle's tuition for a couple of years. This eased the psychological stress she was facing in her first semester in school. She was exhilarated when she held in her hands for the first-time enough money to pay her tuition *and* buy food. On her way back to school, she sat quietly on the bus, but her mind wasn't still. She was singing songs of joy in her heart.

"Come and join me; sing alleluia!
Jehovah Jireh has done me well!
Come and join me; sing alleluia!
Jehovah Jireh has done me well!"

That moment marked a big turnaround for Bayonle. Things were getting better for her. At last, some light appearing at the end of the tunnel.

Moving on, Peter is one of Bayonle's paternal half-brothers. He had relocated to Canada in the late eighties due to constant Academic Staff Union of Universities strikes in Nigeria. He was an engineering student back then and moved to Canada to study. However, he came to Nigeria to visit in the summer of 1996. When he did, he took Bayonle and her two nieces to one of the most expensive restaurants in Ibadan. There was so much food to eat, so many options! Bayonle opted for fried rice, chicken, coleslaw, and cheesecake for dessert. That was the first time she'd ever eaten coleslaw. The colours on the plate were so inviting: red cabbage, green cabbage, carrots, purple onions, and yellow bell peppers. Each bite of the slaw was creamy and crunchy. Back then, only the middle and upper class could afford the food she ate at the restaurant that day. As you can see, that day was utterly memorable.

Peter's visit came when Bayonle's tuition was due. So, he too rescued her by not only paying the tuition but giving her spending money. Bayonle was relieved by Peter's generosity. She could concentrate in class without having to worry about where her next meal would come from or how she would pay her tuition. A few days later, Peter returned to Canada.

Sylvester is Bayonle's oldest living paternal half-brother. He lived in Lagos when Bayonle was younger but came to visit Michael a few times during her elementary school and high-school days. Sylvester's visits would usually only span a few hours. In her final year at the midwifery school, Bayonle caught up with Sylvester at Agnes's place, and he gave Bayonle his address and phone number. He also gave her some money. Interestingly, just a day before their meeting, Bayonle had attended a prayer meeting in church, during which the pastor asked the congregation to pray for divine connection. In this prayer meeting, Bayonle asked God to send destiny helpers to her. Later, she believed the answer to her prayer was her reconnection with Sylvester. Not only did he pay her tuition for her final year, he also assisted her with her final-year school project.

Typewriters were the only machines easily accessible to students in those days. But after Bayonle finished writing her final project, Sylvester gave it to his secretary, who used a computer and colour printer to finish the job. The end product was beautiful; all the bar charts and pie charts came out so brightly coloured. This made Bayonle's research project stand out among her peers. Unbeknownst to the external examiner, the use of the computer wasn't Bayonle's idea, so the examiner wondered why other students hadn't used a computer like Bayonle had. She was awarded the highest grade.

After her graduation from the School of Midwifery in March 1997, she worked in a private hospital for a year. This helped her save up for the next chapter of her life. Finally, on March 15, 1998, she continued on to the University College Hospital Ibadan, School of Nursing for her post-basic nursing program. By this point, she had toughened up and mastered how to thrive on her own. While in school full-time, she worked part-time for a while to support herself financially. She cherished her financial independence, but when her income came up short, her older siblings stepped up and bailed her out again.

Sam, Bayonle's friend also benefited from the kindness of a destiny helper. Sam's father died unexpectedly when she was six years old. He was in a ghastly vehicle accident and died instantly. He left behind Sam, her brother, Paul, who was two years old, and their mother, Anna, who had always been a stay-at-home mom. Unfortunately, their father did not have life insurance. Their extended family could not help much as they too had their own financial problems. The loss was so hard on the family, and especially Anna, that she went into a severe depression. It was so bad she could not leave the house.

Life was very difficult for Sam and her family. By the age of ten, Sam had become Anna's caregiver and Paul's nanny. They lived in one bedroom in an eight-room bungalow. They shared a latrine and a bathroom with ten other tenants. Just like the house Bayonle grew up in, each tenant's kitchen was the small space in front of their room. Sam's family went to bed on an empty stomach so many times. With their mother being sick and unable to work, some of the neighbours would bring them food, and once in a while, Sam's extended family would give them a little money. Those were the only times they did not go to bed hungry. But all that changed when Sam, at fifteen, met her destiny helpers at church.

John and Bose were a young couple who attended the same church as Sam and her family. They had been watching Sam and her family for a while, and Bose could tell that this family needed help. Bose too came from humble beginnings, and she could read all the signs of poverty in Sam's family. She spoke to John about it, and they decided they would ask Sam's mother, Anna, if Sam could come live with them. They both had good jobs and lived in a comfortable three-bedroom house. Anna didn't disappoint them; they knew she would say yes.

John and Bose became Sam's destiny helpers. She moved in with them. They helped her through her education and even sponsored her wedding. Sixteen years later, Sam still keeps in touch with John and Bose. They understood Sam's situation because Bose also had it rough growing up, and she was helped by God-sent angels who didn't know her from Adam. So, Bose and John decided to pay it forward by being Sam's destiny helpers.

Sam's brother, Paul, eventually developed an interest in photography. Thanks to Sam's positive influence, he raised funds, and at the age of fifteen, he bought his first camera from a secondhand store. He started by taking pictures of his friends and schoolmates, and in a few months, he became well-known in his neighbourhood. People would invite him to do photoshoots. By the time he was seventeen, he was shooting birthday parties, weddings, and more. He used the money he was making from his photography business to feed himself and Anna.

Unfortunately, Anna died of her illness at the age of forty-six. As Sam and Paul grieved the loss of their mother, they decided they didn't want history to repeat itself. They chose not to shut down; they embraced everyone that reached out to them. They received help from people around them in the community: neighbours, family, school, and the church. Today, Sam and Paul are both married and doing well.

Asande, a young, registered nurse, relocated to Australia from Africa. She was a Christian in Africa; so, she joined one of the local churches in her new city. One of the church elders, Fred, who has been supporting missionaries abroad for years, took a special interest in Asande. One day, Fred heard that Asande needed a laptop so she could connect with her family back home. Fred asked her how much the laptop she wanted cost, and Asande said, "$700." Fred said he would give her the money on Thursday, when they'd meet at church for Bible study.

Asande was shocked that someone would give her that much money. She consulted her older brother in Ontario, who discouraged her from accepting the gift because the man might have an ulterior motive. Thursday came and Fred offered Asande a white envelope with $700 in it. Asande, having listened to her brother, didn't waste any time and told Fred nicely to keep his money. It's worth noting that Fred was in his early eighties at the time and had a lot of money; all he wanted to do was help a fellow Christian sister. So Fred was disappointed, and Asande could see embarrassment written all over his face. In this instance, it would have been helpful for her to remember, "For all who are led by the Spirit of God are children of God," (Romans 8:14 NLT).

The next few days would be a time of deep revelation for Asande. Asande has been a Christian from childhood. She learned to study the Bible, trust God, take everything to God in prayer, and listen for his direction. Unfortunately, Asande did not pray about Fred's offer or ask God what to do. Instead, she talked to her brother and took his advice. The Spirit of God reprimanded Asande for not asking for divine guidance on the matter. God told her he had prepared Fred to be her destiny helper in Australia; someone that would help her settle down in her new home.

After this revelation, Asande cried to God for forgiveness and asked for a second chance. God answered her prayer when Asande approached Fred after church service the next Sunday, apologized for her actions, and asked if he could give her the money. Surprisingly, the money was still in the same envelope when he brought it to Asande the second time. This would be the beginning of Fred's financial support of Asande. Asande was thankful for having been given a second chance because not everyone who misses an opportunity gets another.

A few years later, Fred died peacefully in his sleep. Asande was shocked when she heard the news of Fred's death because they had spoken via video call the day before his death. Asande had moved to a bigger city by then, but she always stayed in touch with Fred. She was one of many who spoke at Fred's funeral and let it be known that she was a benefactor of Fred's kindness and generosity and that she would miss him terribly.

Asande has now been in Australia for fifteen years and has been helping immigrants like herself settle in Australia. Not only that, but she also helps everyone that the Spirit of God tells her to help regardless of their background, race, colour, or religion. She was helped by her destiny helper, Fred. Now she's paying it forward.

13

Parental Protection

No matter what evil might come one's way to be loved is to be protected.[25] — Kate Morton

I cannot think of any need in childhood as strong as the need for a father's protection. — Sigmund Freud

To protect means "to cover or shield from exposure, injury, damage, or destruction, "according to the Merriam-Webster Dictionary.[26]

One role of a parent is to protect their children from things such as poverty, sexual abuse, and the damage that follows. Unfortunately, Bayonle wasn't protected from these; nevertheless, she determined she would never allow her children to experience what she experienced. So now that she has her own children, she watches them like an elephant. Elephants are known to protect their young from predators. She started to educate them about those most important issues right from their toddler years.

25 Morton, Kate, *The Clockmaker's Daughter*, Goodreads, Retrieved from https://www.goodreads.com/quotes/9575478-no-matter-what-evil-might-come-one-s-way-to-be

26 "Protect," *Merriam-Webster Dictionary*, Retrieved May 24, 2022, from https://www.merriam-webster.com/dictionary/protect

Here are some of the important lessons parents should teach their children:

- how to set boundaries
- body part names and which ones are private
- what appropriate touch and inappropriate touch are
- what good play and bad play are
- how not to allow anyone to touch them inappropriately
- how to say no
- how to recognize bait traps

One of the most important things Bayonle learned about when she was a child was metaphorical fire. Metaphorical fire is a side effect one experiences as a result of abuse. Bayonle learned that one must contain the fire. If a fire is not contained, it will spread and cause a lot of damage and may even take lives. Part of protection is to protect victims. You don't want a victim of trauma to hurt themselves or others. Bayonle was a victim of sexual abuse; and because her trauma wasn't contained, she started to show younger kids the ropes. If not for Mrs. Ade's intervention, the fire of lust Bayonle had carried in her could have smouldered and spread to those kids she was caring for, and then other kids, and then more kids until it became wild and uncontainable. Lust is contagious!

There was no awareness of sexual abuse and predators and personal protection when Bayonle was young. There was no internet, and there were no helplines to call. Things have changed now; the world is evolving, and help is available. Just as parents play a significant role in protecting their children from evil and dangers, children also need to take care of themselves. Once they're capable of making decisions, they must begin to develop the power within them: the power of choice, the power to say no when one needs to say no, and the power to seek help. There are resources in most schools in developed countries. There are social workers, school counsellors, and child protective services that older children can turn to when they need help. Use the helplines available in your locality.

Though available resources may differ from country to country, or there may be a lack of reliable resources for victims of child abuse where you are, there is always someone in your life you can trust and talk to, whether in your home, school, neighbourhood, church, or police services.

Let's not forget the remaining aspects of protection. Just as it's a parent's responsibility to protect their children from abuse, it's equally their responsibility to protect their children from poverty. The effect of poverty on child development is detrimental. It can lead to chronic illness, depression, toxic stress, and substance abuse. Toxic stress disrupts brain structure and increases the risk of developing poor physical, behavioural, social, emotional, and cognitive health.[27] Bayonle's family lived well below the poverty line. This initiated her stress and fatigue.

The discussion concerning finances should start before marriage. Each party should have an internal discussion with themselves about how to plan for the future and how to be financially independent before marriage. Next—before marriage—a couple needs to discuss when they want to have children, how many children they want to have, and how they will provide for their children. Premarital financial counselling is also advised as it will help couples plan for their future

27 Francis, Lucine, DePriest, Kelli, Wilson, Marcela, and Gross, Deborah, "Child Poverty, Toxic Stress, and Social Determinants of Health: Screening and Care Coordination," *The Online Journal Of Issues In Nursing*, 23, no. 3 (2018): 2, https://doi.org/10.3912/OJIN.Vol23No03Man02)

family.[28]

Finally, it's also a parent's responsibility to protect their children from stressors. Children deserve to grow up in a peaceful and loving environment to protect them from mental and emotional abuse. They need stability and security, and they need guidance and support—from two parents. Hand-in-hand with that goes a parent's need to understand a child's fundamental needs at each stage of development. That knowledge would better equip parents to see the signs of trauma in their children. Bayonle believes it is integral for parents of children who have experienced trauma to be well-informed on this subject to be able to protect their children from further abuse such as bullying. Parents always need to be on guard, watchful, and available.

God Factor

I want to end this section on protection with this nugget for thought.

Does it make sense if one sees a car and concludes that the car made itself or that it just appeared from no particular source? What if the car developed a major problem that a regular mechanic couldn't fix? What would happen to the car? The logical answer is it would be sent to the manufacturer for diagnosis and repair; hence, the car has a creator.

God is the creator of human beings.

We all need God at all times.

When you're doing well, you need God.

---

28 Pace, Rachael, "How a Lack of Communication in Marriage can Affect Relationships," Marriage.com, Updated November 20, 2020, https://www.marriage.com/advice/communication/lack-of-communication-in-marriage/

When you're struggling, you need God.

When you're happy, you need God.

When you're anxious or depressed, you need God.

During trials and temptation - you need God.

You will always need God; we all do.

For you to fulfill your purpose in life exactly the way God wants, you need to be anchored to Him. God is the Manufacturer we all need to turn to when we need fixing.

> *Those who live in the shelter of the Most High will find rest in the shadow of the Almighty. This I declare about the Lord: He alone is my refuge, my place of safety; he is my God, and I trust him. For he will rescue you from every trap and protect you from deadly disease* (Psalms 91:1-3 NLT).

There is love, safety, protection, and hope in the everlasting arms of God. All you need to do is run into His arms and enjoy the warmth of His love.

PART 3

PRESERVATION

14

The Vacuum

There's a God-shaped vacuum in the heart of every [person] which cannot be filled by any created thing, but only by God, the Creator, made known through Jesus.[29] *— Blaise Pascal*

As you've seen from the previous chapters in this book, emptiness, hopelessness, and loneliness robbed Bayonle of so many things, including her confidence. She had an enormous vacuum in her heart that none of her support people could fill. She often felt the whole world was against her, that no one cared about her. The longing for acceptance, companionship, and love milked her dry. Does this resonate with you? On many occasions, she had to choose between using her body to get what she needed and leaning on God for sustenance. She had to choose between embracing a destructive lifestyle and turning to God, who could heal her spirit, soul, and body. She chose the latter. And she never once regretted her choice.

Bayonle has watched people—young and old—drown in the deep end. These were people who were traumatized in their childhood due to daddy/mommy issues, poverty, abuse,

29 Towns, Elmer, "Is God Fair to Answer the Prayers of Some People and Not Others?" In *Ten Questions about Prayer Every Christian Must Answer*, 33–45, Nashville, TN: B&H Publishing Group, 1999, Ten Questions about Prayer Every Christian Must Answer (liberty.edu)

or molestation. When friends, family, or preachers told them to bring their pain to God, they would yell at those trying to help them, saying they didn't want anybody talk to them about God. Some folks who needed God's help would ask questions like "Where was God when my abuser raped me? Where was God when I had no food to eat? Where was God when the landlord threw our things out because we could not afford rent? Where was God when I was homeless?" The questions are endless! No matter how hard people try to explain to sufferers that God is not responsible for all the evil people encounter in the world, some just can never accept that. In the end, everything boils down to the choices people make. God is always there; all we need to do is connect with him.

God did not wake an abuser up and whisper to their ears that they should go touch an innocent child inappropriately. Some abusers even fight with the evil voice within them.

In her early twenties, Bayonle started hearing a strange voice in her head that said, "You will fall. You will fall," whenever she walked up the stairs. This voice woke her up one afternoon and asked her to leave the room and go out onto the street. So she did get up and did leave the room, but yet another small voice told her not to obey the first voice. *Was she going crazy? she wondered.*

Bayonle's deliverance finally appeared one day not long later. When she read Psalm 121, verse 3 stood out to her. "He will not allow your foot to be moved; He who keeps you will not slumber." She pondered upon this verse. It soon became the weapon she used to conquer the voice that said, "You will fall. You will fall," whenever she walked up the stairs. She would respond "God will not allow my foot to be moved. I will not fall." And that's how the voice stopped. There's power in the word of God!

No one and nothing can fill that vacuum in your heart. Meth, cocaine, heroin, marijuana, alcohol, other mind-altering substances, sex, gambling, etc., cannot fill this vacuum. They may dull your pain temporarily, but none of these substances can fix you. A round spike does not fit in a rectangular hole; they just don't match.

When cars need servicing or repair, we take them to the mechanic. And there are times when that doesn't work, so you may need to take your vehicle to the dealership or the manufacturer. Similarly, you need to go back to God who is your Maker for repair, reboot, recharging, or replacement of the part of your life that needs fixing.

15

The Beginning of Bayonle's New Life

"Before I formed you in the womb I knew you; before you were born I sanctified you; I ordained you a prophet to the nations." —
Jeremiah 1:5 NKJV

There's a purpose for everything we see around us. You're reading this book for a purpose, whether it is to learn new things, for leisure, or for self-development. The stove in your kitchen has a purpose. Your car has a purpose. These are non-living things. If they have a purpose for why they were manufactured, why won't you and I?

The Creator made you so you can fulfill a particular purpose in life. You're a unique human being; your fingerprints are distinct. Yours are different from other people's fingerprints. You're very special to God; that's why He formed you in a unique way. Once you can establish the fact that you're not in the world by accident, discovering your purpose is not far-fetched.

Bayonle's Escape Routes

Keep these words in mind throughout the following section: "Blessed be the God and Father of our Lord Jesus Christ, the Father of mercies and God of all comfort, who comforts us in all our tribulation, that we may be able to comfort those who are in any trouble, with the comfort with which we ourselves are comforted by God," Apostle Paul (II Corinthians 1:3-4 NKJV).

People with traumatic pasts like Bayonle shouldn't have to suffer from the pain of their past or their mistakes forever. Instead, they can take the opportunity to learn from them and heal. From there, survivors can help others with similar struggles. Bayonle was often at a crossroads in early adulthood where before her was a maladaptive coping mechanism or a healthy coping mechanism. Fortunately, she chose the latter.

Bunmi was bullied in her high-school days because of her height and acne. Does this resonate with you? She was the tallest in her class. She broke out with severe acne when she was fifteen. At first, she became insecure and was too conscious of her looks. Bunmi was raised in a Christian home, and she had accepted Jesus as her Lord and Saviour when she was twelve years old. So, instead of allowing what the bullies said to control her life, with the help of her parents, she took solace in the word of God. She would look at herself in the mirror and say, "I'm the image of God. God says I'm good and beautiful, so I am. I'm who God says I'm. I'm beautiful!" She would thank God every day for making her beautiful. She became so confident that anytime the bullies told her she was ugly, she would respond with, "I'm beautiful because God says I am." When the bullies watched her grow in her positivity, they gave up tormenting her. There's power in positive affirmations. Negative words are unpleasant to your ears and poison to your soul, so don't absorb others' negative words; instead, reject them. You can reject them by saying, "What you just said now is incorrect. I was made in the image and likeness of God. God is good, so I'm good. God is beautiful, so, I'm beautiful. That's the truth!" Bunmi would always say these words in her heart, and as time went by, she became bold enough to speak them to the bullies. You have power over what you allow in your life.

Above all, Bunmi constantly prayed to God to give her the right words to say to the bullies. It worked! She still has acne in her thirties despite trying everything from cosmetics to medical management. But she's grown into a confident woman, an entrepreneur, a wife, and a mother of two beautiful children.

There are so many people in the world that turn to God to escape their bullies. Equally, there are people who embrace unhealthy coping mechanisms to escape being bullied. Dupsy was husky growing up. Her peers and the adults around her teased her about her weight. When she couldn't take it anymore, she developed an eating disorder called anorexia nervosa. Does this resonate with you? The same people that bullied her about being overweight then teased her about her thin appearance. Over time, she developed social anxiety. She spent her early adult life nursing this disorder, going in and out of the hospital with complications of anorexia. She often suffered from anemia, dehydration, bloating, constipation, diarrhea, irregular heartbeat, and more.

After years of therapy, Dupsy overcame her eating disorder, and gradually, her social anxiety. Unfortunately, she developed a different bad habit, substance misuse, to cope with motherhood and a midlife crisis. Does this resonate with you?

There are so many lessons to learn from Bunmi's story. Her initial reaction to being bullied was just how most people would react. She became overly sensitive and insecure about her face. However, she allowed her faith to trump her situation. She accepted help from her parents. She studied the word of God and repeated the beautiful names God calls her. She discovered her identity in Christ. She refused to answer the name her community wanted to paste on her. She refused "ugly" but embraced "good" and "beautiful" because that's what God says she is. She was timid initially, but she became confident and able to confront her fears with the power of prayer and the word of God.

In the quest for answers, we always ask why did this or that happen? Why me? When the answers we're desperately seeking are not in sight, we're disappointed. Day after day, so many questions filled Bayonle's mind for so long, until one day the answers came. It happened in 2005 when she turned thirty. By then, she was married with two children. She was on a bus returning from Lagos to Ibadan where she lived. She sat by the window, looking at the beautiful sky every now and then and the images out the front window. Her mind started to play various scenes of her life: the abuse, her struggles with lust, and the poverty that affected every aspect of her life.

Then a soft voice interrupted her mind's wandering. "Look at gold. It takes a lengthy process to refine gold. The extraction process involves drilling, blasting, hauling, crushing, leaching, and processing. Only then is the gold-rich mud poured into a refinery furnace and heated to 2,000 degrees Fahrenheit (1,093 degree Celsius). After this prolonged process, the gold finally becomes bright and pure. Muddy gold has no beauty, but once it passes through fire, its glory is revealed." On Bayonle's journey, she entered crushed but came out whole. This is because God took the pieces and refined, remoulded, and reshaped her. She went through hell; God used it to purify her. Impurities are easy to remove from a metal once the metal melts. The only way to do this is by passing the metal through fire. All the fire that Bayonle passed through was to beautify her life, not to destroy her.

Next, the voice referred to a plant analogy. It takes about

six to ten weeks to take many of the vegetables we eat from seed to harvest such as spinach, kale, and potatoes. And though you can harvest waterleaf within four weeks, perennial crops such as cocoa take longer from seed to harvest: it takes three to five years. And the harvest continues from generation to generation. Patience is the key!

Bayonle's father, Michael, died at the age of 113. He inherited a cocoa farm, and the farm was inherited by another generation after his passing. Unfortunately, Michael didn't enjoy the proceeds from the cocoa farm. This is partly because he didn't stay and work the farm. His passion was goldsmithing, so that was what he devoted his entire life to. His cousins worked the farm and kept the proceeds for themselves.

Perhaps Bayonle's story is similar to yours. You may not be able to change your past, but you can change the narrative now and determine what you want your future to look like. The power lies within you. You're stronger than you think! Like some other victims of abuse, Bayonle took one day at a time, and at the end, so many factors came into play to allow for her healing and recovery. Here are some of them:

- **Venting**: Many times, Bayonle would express her fear, pain, and other concerns to God in prayer. Then, she was absolutely convinced that God was the only one she could run to for protection and sustenance. Sometimes, she would even leave the hostel, go to the school in the evening, and cry to God. She liked the peace and quiet when no one else was there. It was a private sanctuary for her. She would tell God about the way things were. To her, that was conversing with God. Bayonle grew up with a popular saying: "A problem shared is a problem solved." She believed that God heard her anytime she shared her problems with Him. Oftentimes, she can still hear a small voice saying,

"Don't be afraid. I'm with you. You'll make it. Your future is bright." She felt the presence of her Heavenly Father in the face of her fear as she said to herself, "Bayonle, don't be afraid." Then before she knew it, her fear dissipated. She ruminated, "With God on my side, I can move mountains. I can defeat Goliath!" Life's challenges are bound to happen; in fact, the word of God says when, not if, we pass through these challenges, God will be with us: "When you go through deep waters, I will be with you. When you go through rivers of difficulty, you will not drown. When you walk through the fire of oppression, you will not be burned up; the flames will not consume you" (Isaiah 43:2 NLT).

- **Counselling**: There were no professional counselling services in any of Bayonle's schools. Never did she ever hear of any group or organization for children of divorce, victims of childhood sexual abuse, or childhood poverty survivors during her school years. Bayonle relied on informal counselling from teachers, church leaders, and older siblings who had similar life experiences as her. Knowing that others had walked the same path served as solace for her. Bayonle knows that everyone who came into her life during her healing journey did a wonderful job. They helped her build self-confidence and feel good about herself.
- **Service**: Bayonle volunteered in the church choir. This kept her busy. She also attended Bible study and prayer meetings every week. As the saying goes: "An idle hand is the devil's workshop." Not only did this occupy her mind and spirit with the word of God through her Bible study with others, but it also helped shape her character and social skills.
- **School**: Bayonle was fortunate to have a formal education, although it wasn't without struggle. School

activities and clinicals (practicums) helped her stay focused and engaged. She knew education could provide an escape route from poverty. Moreover, her quest for security kept her moving forward despite all the obstacles in her way. It was Bayonle's firm belief that if she became financially successful, she could not only send her future children to school, but she could also help other children whose parents couldn't afford to send them to school. Knowledge is power; she wanted to be empowered to stand against child abuse and molestation. Education gives a voice to the voiceless. She wanted to be that voice that could help victims, that could help those who had turned to drugs for succour due to their traumatic childhood. She even wished she had the power to stop them from ingesting the "slow poison" in the first place.

- **Bible Study**: She learned the importance of studying and meditating on the word of God when she was in high school. This helped her to know more about God and hold onto His promises. One can grasp a clear picture of the enormity of God's love simply by studying and meditating on the Scriptures. Through continuous fellowship and prayers, one can have the experiential knowledge of His love. This is exactly what happened to Bayonle. Her life was transformed when she realized that God loves her and watches over her. The word of God eased her path. She transitioned from living in the thick darkness of isolation, depression, fear, anxiety, and poverty into living a life full of hope and the love of God. She's no longer afraid of what may come her way; instead, she allows the greatness of God to saturate her heart, knowing full well that as long as God is with her, then nothing can destroy her. Life's challenges are still hard, but God is greater and stronger than any situation and circumstance.

- **Mindset**: Bayonle began her healing journey with a fixed mindset, but gradually, with counselling, self-determination, self-development, and community support, she transitioned into a growth mindset. A fixed mindset creates limitations whereby people believe their talents and intelligence are fixed traits. People with this mindset accept every challenge of life as a complete failure and can't see what can be done or changed to fix the problem. In a study conducted by social psychology researcher, Carol S. Dweck highlighted some of the typical things people with a fixed mindset said when minor life challenges stared them in the face:

- "Everyone is against me."
- "God hates me."
- "People are out there to get me."
- "Life's unfair and my efforts are useless."

Words are powerful! We can use words to create internal and external positivity around us. On the other hand, we can use words to destroy dreams, character, talent, and potential in ourselves and others.

Initially, Bayonle allowed her foundation, her upbringing, and poverty to define the heights she could reach in life. Over time, she started to shed the false ideas and came to believe in the power of growth and possibility.

In a growth mindset, people believe their basic strengths and talents can improve through hard work, thorough self-assessment, planning, and self-evaluation coupled with support from others.[30]

- **Self-love**: When Bayonle embraced the love of God, she learned about self-love. She realized the importance of loving herself and the little girl in her. Bayonle came to accept and appreciate all these aspects of loving herself:
- She likes to pamper herself.
- She stands up for herself when she has to.
- She doesn't have to prove anything to anyone.
- She chooses her friends carefully.
- She's unapologetically herself; she doesn't compare herself to others.
- She enjoys "me time."
- She enjoys physical activities.
- She's truthful with herself and accepts that both good and bad, ups and downs are part of life.
- She sees every challenge or disappointment as an opportunity to learn and grow.
- She knows her limitations and accepts that she can't control some things that happen in life, but she can control how she reacts to them.
- Her philosophy is that for every problem, there's a solution. There's always a way out if one looks closely.
- **Sharing her story**: Bayonle shares her story with individuals and groups going through similar trauma to what she experienced growing up and with survivors in various stages of their healing journey. As she helps these people, she enjoys the feeling of freedom that comes with sharing her story. Being vulnerable with others plays a huge

30 Dweck, Carol. S, *Mindset: The New Psychology of Success*. Ballantine Books, 2007, Penguin Random House Digital, Inc., 2016, https://www.penguinrandomhouse.com/books/44330/mindset-by-carol-s-dweck-phd/

part in her healing!

- **Giving thanks**: Thankfulness is one of the healthy ways Bayonle copes, both during her challenges and on her healing journey. This was especially important when she became a young adult. She believed her misfortunes could be worse. She experiences unspeakable joy whenever she gives thanks. Moreover, thankfulness helped her develop into a strong and independent woman.

16

A Discuss About Temptation and Unhealthy Outlets

No temptation [regardless of its source] has overtaken or enticed you that is not common to human experience [nor is any temptation unusual or beyond human resistance]; but God is faithful [to His word—He is compassionate and trustworthy], and He will not let you be tempted beyond your ability [to resist], but along with the temptation He [has in the past and is now and] will [always] provide the way out as well, so that you will be able to endure it [without yielding, and will overcome temptation with joy]. — Apostle Paul (1 Corinthians 10:13 AMP)

Bayonle's mind became a battlefield as she continued on her healing journey. The journey wasn't easy; it was long! To her, healing is continuous. For a long time, she struggled with lust and images she had seen when she had at one time watched pornography that would not let her rest. Those images continued to play in her head for a very long time. Her triggers are provocative movie scenes. These incite lust in her mind. It's true that the eyes are the gate to the mind. Don't look at anything you don't want to remember. As the book of Proverbs suggests, "Guard your heart above all else, for it determines the course of your life" (Proverbs 4:23 NLT).

Whenever lustful thoughts flood her mind, she responds with, "Get behind me, Satan. This thought is not healthy, it's not godly, and it's not beneficial." Then she allows Philippians 4:8 guide her thoughts:

> Finally, brethren, whatever things are true, whatever things are noble, whatever things are just, whatever things are pure, whatever things are lovely, whatever things are of good report, if there is any virtue and if there is anything praiseworthy—meditate on these things (NKJV).

In essence, she uses the word of God and prayer to combat her temptations. She asks God to help her as she can't lean on just her own strength, wisdom, knowledge, or ability. Moreover, she tries as much as possible not to expose herself to triggers.

Musak was introduced to masturbation and pornography by his friends in grade ten. Musak grew up in church; he prayed with his family twice a day and attended church every Sunday and Bible study every Tuesday. He was molested by their housemaid from age eight to twelve. The maid would expose herself and ask him to touch her; she would also touch him inappropriately. She warned Musak not to tell anyone because if he did, she, Musak, and his parents would die. Thus, the seed of lust was planted in him. Fortunately for Musak, the maid was let go when he turned twelve. But unfortunately, the damage had been done. When he was in grade ten, Musak heard some of his peers talking about pornography and masturbation in the locker room one day; out of curiosity, he decided to explore. This was how Musak's nightmare began.

Despite Musak's parents preaching against lust of the flesh, Musak lost control of his impulses. He watched pornography and masturbated every day. Then it progressed to masturbating three times a day. In his college days, he started having dreams of having sex with strange beings and experimenting with everything he saw in the pornography videos. Eventually, his obsession progressed to masturbating seven times a day or more. Whenever he saw a lady in public, he would have lustful thoughts about her. His actions became involuntary; he had no self-control. At this point, Musak admitted the demon of lust had finally possessed him.

For a long time, Musak continued to suffer in silence. He couldn't share his struggles with anyone. When it got to the point where he felt he was going crazy, he started calling on God in prayer: "Whoever calls on the name of the Lord shall be saved" (Romans 10:13 NKJV). He held upon those words and continued to pray every day until his deliverance came. It was a few weeks after his first SOS to God that he became bold enough to share his struggles with his parents. They didn't judge him; instead, they embraced him and prayed with him and cast the demon out of his life.

Musak got rid of all his triggers: pornography CDs, photos, and other materials that could make him relapse. He surrounded himself with accountability partners that he could call anytime he had lustful thoughts. He didn't have access to a trained therapist, but he surrounded himself with positive influencers. His church worked with him and supported him on his journey. They prayed with him and encouraged him to speak the word of God whenever temptation came knocking. One of the Bible verses he prayed regularly was, "Therefore submit to God. Resist the devil and he will flee from you" (Romans 10:13 NKJV). Anytime a lustful thought came to him, he would pray: "I resist you, you demon of lust. Get out of my heart in Jesus's name. I refuse to think about dirty images. I declare, my thoughts are good, true, godly, pure, lovely, just, and worthy of praise in Jesus's name." In the depths of his struggles, he would say this prayer many times a day. He considered that prayer his therapy and medication. Gradually, the desire to masturbate or watch pornography faded away.

A few years later, Musak got married. Today, Musak and his wife are the senior pastors of a Pentecostal church, and they have two children. Musak shares his testimony and helps teenagers, youths, and adults addicted to masturbation and pornography to overcome their temptations. He tells people if he had turned to illicit drugs during his darkest hours, he wouldn't have survived. He was already addicted to pornography and masturbation; substance abuse may have killed him. Recounting how he lost weight, was constantly fatigued, and felt hopeless, Musak confesses substance use would have altered his senses and consciousness, and he may not have been able to send his SOS to God when he had. It was only when he started to sleep with strange beings in his dreams and his masturbation frequency increased to seven times a day that he came to understand that the battle was no longer physical or psychological but spiritual.

> Finally, my brethren, be strong in the Lord and in the power of His might. Put on the whole armor of God, that you may be able to stand against the wiles of the devil. For we do not wrestle against flesh and blood, but against principalities, against powers, against the rulers of the darkness of this age, against spiritual hosts of wickedness in the heavenly places" (Ephesians 6: 10-12 NKJV).

When Musak read these Bible verses, he remembered how their Sunday school teacher had explained it when he was young. The teacher said there are unseen forces that humans have to contend with every day. They're unseen powers of darkness, demons that go back and forth. They're responsible for the evils we see in the world because they're invisible, they influence people's decisions, they suggest destructive ideas, and they use their evil power on their prey to ensure people go against the will of God. They're responsible for the fall of humankind. They manipulated Eve and Adam in the Garden of Eden. Upon that remembrance, Musak felt a bright light came upon him for the first time, for he had been in the dark for a long time. The devil is a strong enemy; we all need strong weapons to overcome him and his strategies.

Read about some of Musak's weapons below. Do you feel they could work for you?

Truth: After his deliverance, Musak became accountable. He refused to live a lie. He knew the moment he told a lie, the demons would come back because sin is their bus pass.

Righteousness: Musak embraced the righteousness of Christ. He became extra careful. He keeps his heart from pollution by being careful of what he watches. Knowing his eyes are the window to his mind, he refrained from watching images that would take him back to his past addiction. Musak intentionally trained his mind to think only about godly, positive, kind, lovely things, things that would edify him and others.

Sharing the good news: Musak is not shy or ashamed about sharing his journey to deliverance and healing with people. He shares the message of the love of God and salvation that Jesus brought to the world with people who care to listen.

Faith: Although Musak can't physically see God, he believes every promise he reads in the Bible and holds on to it, like this one: "Now faith is the assurance (title deed, confirmation) of things hoped for (divinely guaranteed), and the evidence of things not seen [the conviction of their reality—faith comprehends as fact what cannot be experienced by the physical senses]" Hebrews 11: 1 AMP. That's why he could call on the Lord in his crisis and he was delivered. Musak knew the supernatural power of God could set him free from his addiction, so he asked God to heal him and deliver him from his demons. The evidence of Musak's deliverance is the testimony he shares with people today. It's with faith in God and His Promises that Musak can resist the devil whenever he reminds him of his past.

Salvation: Musak gave his life to Christ when he was thirteen. He learned how to study the word of God thereafter. He fell into temptation, but he got up again and asked the Lord for forgiveness and restoration. One of the declarations he professes to the devil is this: "I've surrendered my life to Jesus. He has set me free from your grip. I'm free indeed. Old things are in the past, and I'm a new man." Does this resonate with you? Jesus will restore you. Come back home!

Sword of the Spirit: This is the word of God. Musak uses this weapon daily. The word of God gives him life, hope, peace, rest, strength, and more. He takes the word of God as seriously as food and medicine. The word of God rejuvenated his sick spirit, soul, and body. It dissected his heart, exposed his lust, removed it, and healed him. This can be your weapon too:

> For the word of God is living and powerful, and sharper than any two-edged sword, piercing even to the division of soul and spirit, and of joints and marrow, and is a discerner of the thoughts and intents of the heart (Hebrews 4:12 NKJV).

Prayer: Musak treats prayer seriously. He prays regularly and enjoys the company of his church family. He uses prayer as his communication channel to God. It's his lifeline.

Discernment: Musak took his prayer life to another level by praying to God to give him the ability to discern. Discernment helps him detect danger before it happens. It keeps him out of trouble. He knows when to pray, and he knows when to set boundaries because of his ability to discern.

Do you need deliverance? Perhaps you know that your battle is not physical, just like Musak did, but you don't know what to pray or how to pray. The first step is to ask Jesus to come into your life. Here are some prayer ideas:

1. Give thanks for everything.
2. Praise God for His faithfulness and mercy.
3. Thank God because He answers prayers.
4. Ask for forgiveness of your sins.

To help you further, try some of these prayer examples. They worked for Bayonle, and they can work for you too.

- "And they overcame him by the blood of the Lamb and by the word of their testimony..." Revelation 12:11 NKJV.
  "I cancel every evil plan against my life and destiny by the blood of Jesus."
- "Assuredly, I say to you, whatever you bind on earth will be bound in heaven, and whatever you loose on earth will be loosed in heaven" (Matthew 18:18 NKJV).
  "I bind every power working against the will of God for my life, in Jesus's name."
- "For the weapons of our warfare are not carnal but

mighty in God for pulling down strongholds, casting down arguments and every high thing that exalts itself against the knowledge of God, bringing every thought into captivity to the obedience of Christ" (II Corinthians 10:4

"I pull down every stronghold, argument, and every power of darkness speaking evil into my life, in Jesus's name."

"My thoughts and imagination shall please God, in Jesus's name. I will not think, see, hear, or do what the devil wants me to think, see, hear, or do, in Jesus's name.

"Jesus, deliver me from this oppression (and mention them e.g., loss, regression, failure, demonic attack, etc.)."

• "And whatever you ask in My name, that I will do, that the Father may be glorified in the Son. If you ask anything in My name, I will do it" (John 14:13

Ask God for physical, emotional, and spiritual healing in any aspect of your life that you feel you need a divine touch.

NOTE: All prayers not quoted from the Bible are courtesy of Eunice Oderinde's blog, *Deliverance Prayers.*[31]

***

For Bayonle, setting boundaries in her personal life has helped her steer clear of emotional attachments to people she shouldn't get too close to. For example, she keeps her distance from males who give her bad signals. If she was in a group setting, she would introduce that person to another male, and

31 Oderinde, Eunice, *Blog, Deliverance Prayers*, Retrieved May 23, 2022, from https://euniceoderinde.blogspot.com/2021/09/deliverance-prayers.html

if she was alone, she would cross the room or leave the room. If she was working on a committee and has to work directly with someone that may be a trigger for her, she would change partners for her own peace of mind. She has seen the light; she doesn't want to fall back into the deep end. A boundary example for others might include those who fall back into their old criminogenic environment after a long rehabilitation for substance addiction or long incarceration simply because they were triggered by the company of their old partners in crime after their release[32]. Does this resonate with you? If you don't staunchly create and enforce personal boundaries to buffer you from your triggers, you'll go from the frying pan to fire.

Tom was introduced to meth in his childhood. His parents were in and out of his life due to their frequent jail time resulting from their lifestyle. They struggled with alcohol and illicit drug misuse, they were always involved in theft and burglary to sustain their lifestyle, and they always ended up in jail. Of course, Tom wound up in the bad company and soon followed in his parents' footsteps. In Tom's family, drug misuse and breaking the law were generational. Soon, Tom found himself in and out of rehab. Unfortunately, he would always go back to the same environment. Tom did not follow through with the plans his therapists and other rehabilitation staff suggested. Eventually, he found himself in and out of jail for assault and more.

It's important for people returning from rehab or jail to surround themselves with positive influencers. Going back to

32 Kirk, David S., "A natural experiment on residential change and recidivism: Lessons from hurricane Katrina," American Sociological Review, 74, no. 3 (June 2009): 484-505, Retrieved May 23, 2022, from https://www.proquest.com/scholarly-journals/natural-experiment-on-residential-change/docview/218829721/se-2?accountid=50383

your old environment and lifestyle could be likened to a dog that always goes back to his vomit. A change of environment is one of the strategies that prevent recidivism.[33]

Another strategy Bayonle found helpful was reading books that support healing and emotional health. Here are some of the books she read:

1. *Battlefield of the Mind* by Joyce Meyer
2. *Healing the Soul of a Woman* by Joyce Meyer
3. *Do It Afraid* by Joyce Meyer
4. *The Longing In Me* by Sheila Walsh
5. *The Pursuit of God* by A. W Tozer
6. *Power of Vision* by Myles Munroe
7. *Understanding Your Potential* by Myles Munroe
8. *Rediscovering Faith* by Myles Munroe
9. *Mindset, the New Psychology of Success* by Carol Dweck
10. *Where is God in My Storm?* by Kenneth Hagin
11. Journals and articles, many of which are referenced in this book

33 Kirk, David S. (2009).

Bayonle's Unhealthy Escape Routes

Bayonle did make some good choices, listened to her destiny helpers, and followed the word of God, but she's still human. She too gave in to temptation and used some unhealthy escape routes at times to ease her pain. Do any of these resonate with you?

Overeating: Bean porridge was one of the cheapest foods, so it fit Michael's budget. She would make bean porridge at least three times a week. That in itself might not sound bad, but on some days, Bayonle would eat so much bean porridge so constantly that her small tummy would enlarge as if she was four months pregnant. She would eat until she had indigestion followed by diarrhea and vomiting. She could tell when her stomach was overfilled, but she did it anyway. It made her feel like she had some control over something in her life. Each time she overate, she regretted it, but then she would go and do it again.

Holding Grudges: Bayonle would take offense to any little thing, even something as small as something a neighbour said to her. So, she would not talk to them for weeks.

Internalizing: Bayonle kept her struggles a secret for a long time. She experienced low energy, loneliness, shame, fear, abandonment, lack of social skills, and low self-esteem for a long time. Though she didn't appreciate any of those feelings, she didn't talk to anyone about them. Perhaps it was because she was afraid, perhaps it was because she didn't know who to talk to, or perhaps it too gave her a measure of control.

Don't continue following your dark path. Don't keep giving in to your temptations. Don't keep diving into your unhealthy escape routes. Use this book and the stories of those in it as your own destiny helper. Remember their struggles and use their examples to avoid your own strife and pain.

17

The Love of Bayonle's Life

Like an apple tree [rare and welcome] among the trees of the forest,
So is my beloved among the young men!
In his shade I took great delight and sat down,
And his fruit was sweet and delicious to my palate.
— Songs of Solomon 2:3 (CEB)

As the saying, "Never say never," goes, Bayonle gave true love a chance in her college days. Her take on marriage began to change after she attended marriage seminars in school and at her local church. She listened to guest speakers and marriage counsellors as they defined the origin and purpose of marriage. She enjoyed listening to the testimonies of couples that had been married for many years, how they managed their differences and settled their conflicts. She began to see that she had a lot to gain if she partnered with someone special in the journey of life. As this passage expresses, "Two are better than one because they have a good reward for their labor. For if they fall, one will lift up his companion," (Ecclesiastes 4:9-10 NKJV).

Bayonle prayed to God constantly because she desperately didn't want history to repeat itself. She didn't want to make a bad decision and marry an abuser or a narcissist. She desired a man who knew and loved God. God is love and a man that loves God will love his wife as he loves himself.

Then one day, Bayonle had the opportunity to meet godly young men in her school fellowship. They became her "burden bearers." They were different from the men she had known in her childhood. This group of young men was not users and abusers like the ones that had taken advantage of her innocence and vulnerability. These were people whom she could talk to and pray with, with no strings attached. Their motives were only genuine, nonsexual love. Strangely enough, none of these Christian brothers asked her out. But out of the blue, John showed up.

During the Easter weekend of 1995, Bayonle's local church ran a weekend-long program that John happened to go to. After the evening program on Saturday, as she was about to rush back to the college hostel with her friend, Yetty, they heard a masculine voice behind them say, "Excuse me." They both turned around. Standing behind them was a tall, handsome man in blue jeans and a grey polo T-shirt, rather a contrast to the choir uniform Bayonle wore while attending this program: a white button-up shirt, black beret, and black flats since she hated heels. He looked like a man on a mission.

The man introduced himself as John and asked to speak to Bayonle. At Bayonle's okay, Yetty left, and John walked Bayonle to the hostel that evening. That was the beginning of their lifetime relationship, though it didn't necessarily come easily on her part.

Bayonle prayed and confirmed through divine revelation that her future with John was bright. People who have surrendered their lives to Jesus and have relationship with him through prayer and studying of the word of God have access to God's leadership and guidance. Prayer is a way of speaking with God. It's a two-way conversation: when a believer speaks to God, God responds. Bayonle prayed a prayer of inquiry before she agreed to marry John. She went to God like a daughter would go to her father for advice or direction, and God told her to go ahead with the relationship. She heard God speak to her heart.

Bayonle saw love, selflessness, humility, and friendliness in John, something she hadn't seen in most men in her childhood. This, coupled with all her church's teachings about marriage, made her embrace the institution of marriage. So on December 18, 1999, Bayonle and John tied the knot. John became a great support on her journey. He helped her during her struggles with her inability to forgive. He reiterated that Jesus forgave us and He wants us to forgive others. With John as her support system, Bayonle was able to forgive the people that hurt her in the past and become an advocate for forgiveness as she reached out to victims of child abuse and poverty. She began to see forgiveness as part of self-love and healing for her wounded soul. John is an agent of peace. He always brings people together for a good cause at work, at church, in the neighbourhood, and among extended family members. And not only is John full of God's love and goodness, but he is also a hard worker and a good provider. John was a banker when they met. Immediately after her graduation, Bayonle got a respectable job in an Ibadan hospital. Together, they could afford a comfortable three-bedroom apartment with all the amenities Bayonle lacked growing up. Then in 2002, they bought their first car. That's what can be achieved when two good people combine forces on the journey of life.

There are many people around the world who are survivors of parental divorce, poverty, and abuse who met their destiny helpers and loving spouses and are doing very well in their respectful homes. Bayonle is lucky to call a few of them friends. God can help you as well and connect you with the right people if you let Him in.

Although Bayonle had it rough growing up, she believes God did not plan the misfortunes she experienced. Instead, God used those experiences that appeared on her life journey to build resilience in her and used them to shape her into the strong and independent woman she has become.

Starting from the early years of their marriage, Bayonle and her husband have opened the door of their home to people in need, regardless of their relationship with Bayonle. They give to the poor around them. Their philosophy is that as everything they have was given to them by God, and as He has shown them unconditional love, they too ought to pay it forward.

18

You Too Can Preserve Your Inner Self

"Are you waiting till the "right" moment when you're finally "done" healing to do something?
Healing is an ongoing process and it is possible to do all the things and be all the things you want to be right now". - Dr. Caroline Leaf[34]

Preserve: To keep alive, intact, or free from decay. — Merriam-Webster Dictionary[35]

You can keep yourself from further trauma. Where are you in your journey now? Your current physical and mental states will determine what you need to do next. You can preserve what you have left in you. This will help in securing your future. Maybe, if you now have children of your own, you can preserve your inner self *and* their future by sharing your story

34 Dr. Caroline Leaf (Apr 27/22). Facebook Post. Retrieved May 28/22 from https://m.facebook.com/story.php?story_fbid=pfbid02A6m-Kt2tQzaZPz94QEMGMBeV5YDpnYRgGx5nzBX3EGPsjyXwYaKABVkLgN7n-JoB9Nl&id=100044135541243

35 "Preserve," *Merriam-Webster Dictionary,* Retrieved May 24, 2002, from https://www.merriam-webster.com/dictionary/preserve

with them, but *only when you're ready*. You must be careful in the way your story is shared. You don't want to share your story just to stir up bitterness, resentment, and vengeance in your children's hearts. Nor do you want to jeopardize their mental health. Nevertheless, you want to share your story so they can learn from it.

Next, accept your emotions. Don't beat yourself up for the way you feel. Remember, given the research findings used throughout this book, you're not the only one that feels this way and other survivors have the same feelings as you. Consider reading some of the books that helped Bayonle. Talk to someone you trust: a friend, a leader, a family member, a professional, anyone who can help you. You may also want to consider joining a support group(s). Ask God to help you! There are many options; you just have to pick the right one for you at this moment.

Once you've made it through that step, then it's time to repair broken bridges and nurture good relationships, but you want to focus on yourself first. So that's where we'll start. Here are some steps to take to preserve your inner self so you can move on to repairing those broken bridges and nurturing those good relationships.

Don't Abuse Yourself!

One of the virtues perpetrators rob their victims of is self-worth. It takes self-love, determination, and help from your support system to recover your self-worth. The good news is you can recover everything stolen from you. Keep these words in mind when self-incriminating thoughts roll in: "The thief does not come except to steal, and to kill, and to destroy. I have come that they may have life, and that they may have it more abundantly," (John 10:10 NKJV).

The perpetrator here is the thief; that is, the devil. Jesus once came to destroy the works of the devil. He came to give you abundant life. As God has plans for you, so also does the devil. Whoever you turn to will determine your outcome. The devil is a killer and a destroyer; whereas, God is the Giver of Life, and His plans for you are good not evil. Don't allow the devil to influence you. Let Jesus help you!

Survivors of traumatic childhoods have the potential to become unintentional self-abusers. If you deny yourself self-love and a good life, you're abusing yourself. If you constantly blame yourself for your past misfortune, you're abusing yourself. If you turn to illicit drugs and/or alcohol for your emotional pain relief, you're abusing yourself. You're not punishing your abuser by embracing a destructive lifestyle; you're only punishing yourself. You need to love yourself enough to say things like this instead:

"You know what, I deserve better. I'll turn a new leaf."
"I'll take good care of myself."
"I'll seek help."
"I need to do this for me."

Don't feel bad for taking care of yourself, for loving yourself. You did nothing to deserve your past trauma, so don't continue to abuse yourself long after your trauma is over.

Self-Development

What are your interests? Find your strengths and talents; develop them and grow with them. Find your purpose in life and pursue it. This will keep you occupied.

Take good care of yourself physically, emotionally, psychologically, and spiritually.

You're not alone! I know this sounds cliché, but truly, others feel the same way you do. You didn't do anything wrong; your abusers were wrong. It's true that your trauma may fully be known to you alone. Perhaps, no one can understand the intensity of your pain—true. You still deserve healing and it's possible.

You're not a fool.
You're not a failure.
You're not a loser.
You're only in transition.

Where you are now is not your destination. You may feel life is unfair or no one likes you, but you're loved beyond measure; that's why you're alive today. If you think you've tried everything and nothing seems to help, look inward: you may find self-development and self-love strategies you hadn't thought of.

19

Triple Hood

Hood: a protective covering for the head and face
— Merriam-Webster Dictionary[36]

No human can function without the brain. It's the centre of one's mental health. It controls all the body's systems and functions such as thinking, feeling, breathing, hearing, seeing, digesting, and more. The list goes on. The brain is the machine that runs all the body's activities; therefore, it must be protected. Vital organs like the brain need to be preserved for the body to function optimally. Equally important is the health of the mind and the heart. In fact, the physical health of an individual impacts their emotional well-being and their spiritual well-being. These health aspects are not isolated. Instead, they are interrelated and interwoven in the overall health of an individual.

For Bayonle, the trauma of parental divorce, childhood sexual abuse, and poverty not only affected her physically, but also psychologically. It was a heavy burden Bayonle carried for many years. As she moved into adulthood, she was able to define the line between lust and love though she struggled

36 "Hood," *Merriam-Webster Dictionary*, Retrieved May 24, 2022, from https://www.merriam-webster.com/dictionary/hood

with building relationships. The fear of being hurt kept her from mingling. As a result, she had to learn to enjoy being by herself as a means of survival. Bayonle thought no one could understand her. It took her a long time to consider even just friendship, but eventually, she figured it out with support from her family and community.

The effects of untreated childhood trauma could be likened to cancer that spreads to other parts of the body. The social, emotional, and psychological aspects of life cannot be healthy if an untreated disease is present. In fact, everything could go wrong if childhood trauma remains untreated. It is also crucial to avoid just scratching the surface when treating deep and interwoven trauma. This can be likened to a doctor that only treats the symptoms without treating the cause.

One of those untreated childhood trauma victims was Bayonle's childhood friend, Johnson, who equally suffered from poverty growing up. His father lost his job when Johnson was in grade eight. His mother's income wasn't enough to sustain their family of eight. His father tried his hand at a few businesses, but none were successful. The family could barely afford two meals a day. Johnson's parents also couldn't afford his school fees. His father took his frustrations out on the children. He became verbally, emotionally, and physically abusive.

One day, Johnson took his friend's advice and tried marijuana. Johnson was seventeen at the time. Unfortunately, the few puffs he took that day set him on a destructive path. He continued to smoke weed, and he became psychotic. He was medically diagnosed with drug-induced psychosis at twenty-four. All efforts to wean him off marijuana proved fruitless.

Johnson married during one of his sober seasons, but he later relapsed. He abused his wife whenever he didn't take his antipsychotic medications. And when his wife could no longer cope, she left him. She waited and hoped and supported Johnson through his many opportunities to go for treatment, but he blew every chance. Johnson's addiction led to his life falling apart. He denied his addiction even when he was sober. He refused to go for therapy. He left rehab many times without completing the treatment and taking his prescribed medications. Johnson's family and friends tried to help him; they didn't give up on him. But Johnson refused to help himself.

One morning, neighbours found Johnson's lifeless body in his room. He was forty-eight. His family and friends knew it was coming given Johnson's lack of motivation to accept help. At the same time, they were devastated by his death. They believed he could have led a good life if he didn't use drugs to numb the pain of his childhood trauma. His ex-wife said he was a good husband and father whenever he was sober. Days, weeks, and years after Johnson's death, there were so many "what ifs" in the hearts and mouths of people closest to him. What if he had completed his treatment? What if he had taken his medications consistently? What if his father hadn't lost his job? What if . . . ?

Moreover, Johnson's death prompted many people to evaluate their own lives and ask themselves some honest questions. His death had been so sudden, as had been the genesis of his problem. His father hadn't seen his job loss coming. Do any of these questions that Johnson's friends and family asked sound familiar?

What do you do when trouble comes?
What do you do if your only source of income disappears?
What do you do if your child starts to misuse drugs?
What do you do if your partner becomes a stranger to you?

What do you do if life becomes unfair?

What do you do if your troubled child or partner refuses help?

What do you do if you can't make ends meet?

Substance abuse is not the answer to any of the questions listed above, nor any other question or problem or challenge. There are nondestructive ways one can manage life's challenges. Some are listed in this book.

A little known or discussed aspect of unhealthy coping mechanisms is overeating. Overeating may feel good for a season but the long-term effects of this can be devastating. Overeating comes with problems of its own, namely regret and obesity. Obese people are more susceptible to high blood pressure, diabetes, heart problems, breathing problems, depression, anxiety, and more diseases and disorders.

Compulsive shopping is another coping mechanism some people use. Some people refer to it as retail therapy. In the case of these victims, whenever something reminds them of their childhood trauma, they go shopping. For some, their childhood trauma stemmed from the struggles associated with poverty. This sort of trauma leads to the development of excessive materialism. Afterward, in the quest to escape from poverty, these victims turn to crime to support their compulsive shopping. To some, this pattern becomes an unstoppable impulse. There are healthier ways of coping with life's problems.

Another common coping mechanism is completely shutting down. Some victims create an imaginary bubble or a cocoon and remain there. They don't want to have anything to do with anyone around them. They don't want to give friendship or relationship a chance. If they're married, their spouses suffer the consequences of their untreated trauma. And when their spouses can no longer cope, they leave.

To the victims of parental divorce, childhood sexual abuse, and poverty: don't allow compulsive shopping, illicit drug use, overeating, prostitution, gambling, and other negative coping mechanisms lead you down a destructive path. You can do better! It's okay if you've tried a healthy approach and it didn't last. It's okay if you've fallen a few times. You can get up again. You can try those healthy strategies again. Or try new ones. Look at what you can do differently to make it work this time. Perhaps you need someone that can hold you accountable. Do you need a life coach? Have you gone for counselling or therapy?

One of Bayonle's unhealthy coping mechanisms was to put herself in a bubble and isolate herself from the rest of the world. This affected her social life adversely. Moreover, Bayonle didn't want to trust any man. She viewed men as the same as the molesters she had encountered in her childhood. Eventually, however, as you read earlier, she came around. She still believes her decision to choose healing over a perpetual broken heart, forgiveness over unforgiveness, and life over death came just in time. Her positive decisions later in life were made possible by the mercy and power of God. She believes she couldn't have made those decisions without divine help. Through the course of Bayonle's healing journey, she summed up all the strategies that helped her into three categories, as this book illustrates: **prevention, protection, and preservation**. Bayonle continues to use the same strategies to help others with similar childhood traumas to hers.

According to Dr. Block, former president of the American Academy of Pediatrics, "Adverse childhood experiences are the single greatest unaddressed public health threat facing the world today."[37] Adverse childhood experiences affect victims' health throughout their lifetime. This can change if parents, guardians, and the government adopt prevention, protection, and preservation strategies.

37 Burke Harris, Nadine, "How Childhood Trauma Effects Health Across a Lifetime," *New York Association of Psychiatric Rehabilitation, Inc.*, September 9, 2014, https://www.nyaprs.org/e-news-bulletins/2015/ted-childhood-trauma-and-health-across-a-lifetime-and-the-public-health-response-necessary#:~:text=In%20the%20words%20of%20Dr,people%2C%20that's%20a%20terrifying%20prospect

20

The Three P's Applied To a Life-Changing Event

Grief is like the ocean. It comes in waves, ebbing and flowing. Sometimes the water is calm, and sometimes it is overwhelming. All we can do is learn to swim. —Vicki Harrison

John and Bayonle, like other married couples, had their own share of life's challenges and struggles during their marriage. Challenges such as job changes, relocation, job loss, and family illness were among some of the issues John and Bayonle dealt with. One of these storms of life shook them to the core.

Something devastating happened eight months after John and Bayonle got married. They became pregnant in January of 2000. They were so happy when they found out they were pregnant. They started shopping for the baby's things immediately. The pregnancy continued to advance as expected. There was no morning sickness and no complications whatsoever. Bayonle remembers how she would daydream about how their lives would be when their son is born. They would set up all the baby's things one day, then a few days later rearrange them, then start all over again. It was fun!

Then in August 2000, Bayonle went for a routine sonogram alone as John was out of town. The sonographer asked her a few questions:

Sonographer: Have you noticed any changes lately?

Bayonle: No.

Sonographer: When was the last time you felt the baby move?

Bayonle: I feel its movement regularly, yesterday to be precise.

At this point, Bayonle became apprehensive, so she asked the sonographer, "Is anything the matter?" The sonographer only said, "You need to take this ultrasound report to your doctor right away."

Why? What could the result be? Why was the sonographer being so dramatic about this ultrasound? This was the third routine ultrasound Bayonle had had. Why was this one so different that the sonographer had suggested I see my doctor that day? The more questions she asked herself, the more afraid she became.

The sonographer put the report in an envelope and gave it to her. As she left the ultrasound room, out of curiosity, she opened the envelope and read the report. Bayonle's head went blank for a few seconds; all of a sudden, she became sweaty and shaky at the same time. What she had read in the ultrasound report had never crossed her mind, not once. She wished John was there with her. The report read "IUD" meaning intra-uterine death. She rushed to the hospital immediately, which happened to be where she worked at the time. She was induced that same day. Everything changed for John and Bayonle that day.

As John and Bayonle grieved the loss of their son, they encouraged and supported each other. They took their pain and sorrow to the Lord in prayer. They couldn't afford to lose each other to physical, mental, or spiritual malaise. Instead, they applied Triple Hood's 3 P's.

Prevention

First, John and Bayonle focused on their physical, mental, and spiritual health. They didn't want unhealthy complications or negative consequences to set in. They knew that if they didn't grieve in a healthy way, things would only get worse. If they didn't take care of their physical and spiritual needs, their mental health would suffer.

Second, John and Bayonle reflected on their blessings regularly. They realized their situation could be worse. For example, what if John had lost both her and the baby? This helped them be intentional about gratefulness. Being thankful is therapeutic! To them, gratefulness was their detox program. The more thankful they were, the more their sorrow and pain lessened. In the long run, they achieved full recovery. They did devotion together every morning, which is a time of prayer and devotional reading. Devotional consists of reading and meditating on the Bible. Sometimes it might just be one Bible verse that gave them the comfort they needed that day. Here is one verse that kept them going: "Rejoice evermore. Pray without ceasing. In everything, give thanks to God, for this is the will of God in Christ Jesus concerning you." (1 Thessalonians 5:16-18 NKJV). And these days, with technology and the internet, one can access the Bible and devotionals online. *Our Daily Bread*, *Open Heavens*, *Daily Manna*, *Insight for Today,* are among many good sites available online.

Third, adequate nutrition is integral. Inadequate nutrition and inadequate fluid intake can lead to dehydration, anemia, hypotension, weakness, an inability to get pregnant, and so on.

Also, when you neglect your physical needs, your emotional and spiritual well-being can be jeopardized. In view of this, John ensured Bayonle ate well and took her vitamins, and she did the same for him.

Fourth, they encouraged each other to sleep adequately. They lived in Nigeria, West Africa at the time. The temperature was always in the double digits (Celsius) there. They would take cold showers in the evening before bed to help them sleep. Lack of sleep is not uncommon with people who are grieving, and the associated complications can result in long-term problems. It can lead to short-term and long-term memory loss, lack of concentration, anxiety, and depression. It also increases the risk of weight gain, Type 2 diabetes, hypertension, a weakened immune system, decreased libido, and more.[38]

Finally, exercise, such as walking, biking, and swimming is uplifting and healthy. For Bayonle and John other physical activities like short and long walks were refreshing. Walking early in the morning or after sunset and feeling the cool breeze lightened their moods; it was like a tonic. There's something divine about the beauty of nature that can pull you out of darkness.

Protection

It's so helpful to have supportive people around when one is grieving. This was one of John and Bayonle's saving graces. Their families and the church community supported them in different but equally helpful ways: they visited, they brought food, they counselled them, and they prayed with them. They were like a protective umbrella. It's important to mention that

38 Watson, Stephanie, and Kristeen Cherney, "Effects of Sleep Deprivation," *Healthline Media*, Updated December 15, 2021, https://www.healthline.com/health/sleep-deprivation/effects-on-body

if Bayonle and John had put up a barrier, there's no way they would have received the support they did from family, friends, colleagues, and their church community.

Some people shut down completely when they're grieving and internalize their pain. Does this resonate with you? I strongly recommend you talk to a professional(s). They can help you and arm you with strategies to bring you back to the world.

Preservation

John and Bayonle always had each other's back, and they came to an understanding that they needed to preserve their relationship so they could enjoy their lives together and build a solid foundation for their unborn children. They checked in on each other regularly. They verbalized their feelings and thoughts. Communication was very important to them then, and it's still important to them now. They knew before they got married that lack of communication in marriage can lead to many problems, such as resentment, emotional disconnection, abuse, money issues, low sex drive, infidelity, and more.[39] Their communication line was and is always open; even when they argue, they always clear the air when they're ready to talk about it, usually on the same day. For the most part, they don't allow the sun to go down before they make up.

Their faith was a weapon Bayonle and John also preserved. Their faith was like a bulb connected to a power source. The light comes on when we press the switch. They believed that as long as they stay connected to God, there will always be

39 Pace, Rachael, "How a Lack of Communication in Marriage can Affect Relationships," *Marriage.com* Updated November 20, 2020, https://www.marriage.com/advice/communication/lack-of-communication-in-marriage/

light. And when the light is on, darkness disappears. They stayed connected to God through prayer, studying, meditating on the word of God, and listening to sermons that speak to their situation. There are great sermons on YouTube about overcoming life challenges, especially the loss of a loved one. Bayonle and John strongly believed that no amount of sorrow could bring their son back. They trusted God would give them another son, so they continued to work toward it.

Everything that Bayonle went through in the past helped her build resilience over the years. Resilience has been a great tool for her. As such, Bayonle and John decided to preserve their resilience. They did this through relaxation, positive thinking, and staying connected to each other.

In June of 2001, their miracle, their healthy baby boy, Isaac, was born. And in 2005, they had their beautiful baby girl, Esther.

***

Fast forward to the present, and as a mother to two young adults, Bayonle is thankful she didn't follow in her father's footsteps in raising her children. Right from the get-go, she resolved over and over again to not adopt her father's parenting style.

Over time, she's learned crucial lessons about the dangers of inflicting physical and emotional pain on a child all in the name of discipline. Extreme physical discipline has serious, long-lasting consequences:

- It will not *teach* the child how to become the person their parents want them to be.
- It can harden the child's heart.
- It can inspire hatred, bitterness, and unforgiveness in

the child.

- It can cause a child to become rebellious.
- It can make the child believe physical abuse is okay.
- It can make the child look for affirmation, validation, affection, and love in the wrong places.
- It can lead to permanent physical disability.
- It can predispose the child to mental illness.
- It can cause a child to become an abuser in the future.
- It can lead to death.[40]

Believe it or not, those aren't all the negative consequences of extreme physical discipline. The list goes on, but you get the idea.

No true parent wants an unhealthy or no relationship with their children in the future. This is why it's important for parents to bring their children up in an atmosphere of love. Correct your children with love! Speak with them instead of using physical punishment to correct every simple mistake they make. Do not take your anger out on your children. You may have been raised in an abusive environment, and while you can't control the past, you can control the present and avoid regret in the future.

40 American Academy of Child and Adolescent Psychiatry, "Physical Punishment," No. 105, Updated March 2018, https://www.aacap.org/AACAP/Families_and_Youth/Facts_for_Families/FFF-Guide/Physical-Punishment-105.aspx

21

Are You Grieving the Loss of Your Friend or Loved One or a Relationship?

A thermometer is used to measure temperature; I have not come across a tool called a "traumameter." That said, the only person that can describe how a trauma victim feels or the degree of the trauma and its effects on the victim's physical, mental, emotional, and spiritual health is the trauma victim themself. People grieve differently. Some grieve longer than others. That doesn't mean those whose grieving periods were shorter than that of their counterparts were less traumatized and vice versa. Everyone deserves to heal—and in their unique way and pace.

Are you struggling through your grieving period? Have you tried any of the tools that helped John and Bayonle during their darkest time? Perhaps you need to take a vacation, go for a massage, watch a movie, or listen to soul-lifting music. You may also want to experiment with nature, such as gardening, outdoor photography, or bird watching. There is joy and a feeling of achievement as you watch plants grow. When you weed your plants, think about any negative things in your life that you need to get rid of. Make a conscious effort to remove all the thorns in your life. When you water your plants, think about what you can do to refresh your spirit, soul, and body. When you add nutrients or fertilizer to your plants, think about the ingredients you need to add to your life that can help you through this period: it could be talking to a friend, going for counselling, or finding a new hobby.

All the childhood trauma Bayonle endured, and the loss of their son, made her draw closer to God to receive strength, power, and grace on her journey. That's not to say there weren't days when she didn't have the strength and courage to leave the house. She could stay indoors for seven days straight, or more. There were days when she would ask why and how did it happen? There were days she would shed tears uncontrollably. There were days she would prefer to be alone, days that she wouldn't want anyone in her personal space, not even her husband. On days when her soul was downcast, she would lift her eyes to her Heavenly Father for comfort. She would pour out her burden to the Lord in prayer. She would listen to songs that would lift her soul. This is one such song:

I'm Trading My Sorrows

I'm trading my sorrows,
I'm trading my shame,
I'm laying them down for the joy of the Lord.
I'm trading my sickness,
I'm trading my pain,
I'm laying them down for the joy of the Lord,
And we're singing.

Yes, Lord; yes, Lord; yes yes, Lord.
Yes, Lord; yes, Lord; yes yes, Lord.
Yes, Lord; yes, Lord; yes yes, Lord, amen.

I am pressed but not crushed,
Persecuted not abandoned,
Struck down but not destroyed.
I am blessed beyond the curse,
For His promise will endure
That His joy is gonna be my strength.
Though the sorrow may last for the night,
His joy comes in the morning.

I'm trading my sorrows,
I'm trading my shame,
I'm laying them down for the joy of the Lord.
I'm trading my sickness,
I'm trading my pain,
I'm laying them down for the joy of the Lord,
And we're singing.

Yes, Lord; yes, Lord; yes yes, Lord.
Yes, Lord; yes, Lord; yes yes, Lord.
Yes, Lord; yes, Lord; yes yes, Lord, amen.[41][42]

As the song implies, Bayonle gave up pain, shame, and sorrow in exchange for the joy that only Jesus can give. Psalms 55:22 says, "Give your burden to the Lord, and he will take care of you …" When Bayonle gave her burden to the Lord,

41 Evans, Darrell, "I'm Trading my Sorrows," Integrity's Hosanna! Music, *Divine Hymns*, Retrieved May 19, 2022, from https://divinehymns.com/lyrics/im-trading-my-sorrows-song-lyrics/

42 Women of Faith, "I'm Trading My Sorrows," YouTube video, Uploaded February 17, 2012, https://www.youtube.com/watch?v=4K1jn-nz0skQ

he took care of her and her burden. The Lord can do the same for you if you give your burden to him. God knows your name and every detail about you. He will help you every step of the way if you open the door of your heart to him.

There's a woman in the Bible (Mark 5:25-34) who suffered from an ailment that caused her to bleed for twelve years. She explored every known cure; unfortunately, nothing worked for her. She went from one doctor to another, but instead of getting better, she deteriorated. Imagine the pain this woman carried for twelve years. She spent all her money trying to treat this terrible ailment. She had nothing left. She ran out of options, and then one day, she heard about Jesus. She thought, "If I can touch his robe, I'll be healed." Her opportunity came when Jesus passed by one day, so she touched Jesus's robe from behind. Immediately, her bleeding stopped. Jesus knew power had transferred from him. He asked the crowd, "Who touched me?" The woman replied, "I did." So Jesus said, "Daughter, your faith has made you well. Go in peace. Your suffering is over." (Mark 5:34 NLT)

You too can touch Jesus through prayer, and he will heal you. No matter how long you've been carrying the pain of your trauma—days, months, or years—Jesus can give you peace. For example, a man in the Bible was helpless; he remained in the same place for thirty-eight years because he was paralyzed. Jesus came to him one day and healed him. The man got up and walked then (John 5:1-10). Jesus can get you onto your feet again. Like that woman in the Bible, maybe you've gone from doctor to doctor, from one therapist to another, with no results. Jesus, the Great Physician, can heal you, remould you, and put you back together again. There's power in the name of Jesus. Call His name; He answers all prayers.

There's a story of another man in the Bible. People called

him a madman' because of his mental illness. Does this resonate with you? Are you called names or stereotyped because of your illness? This story is for you then.

> They arrived on the other side of the sea in the country of the Gerasenes. As Jesus got out of the boat, a madman from the cemetery came up to him. He lived there among the tombs and graves. No one could restrain him—he couldn't be chained, couldn't be tied down. He had been tied up many times with chains and ropes, but he broke the chains, snapped the ropes. No one was strong enough to tame him. Night and day he roamed through the graves and the hills, screaming out and slashing himself with sharp stones.
>
> When he saw Jesus a long way off, he ran and bowed in worship before him, then bellowed in protest, "What business do you have, Jesus, Son of the High God, messing with me? I swear to God, don't give me a hard time!" Jesus had just commanded the tormenting evil spirit, "Out! Get out of the man!"
>
> Jesus said, "Tell me your name."
>
> He replied, "My name is Mob. I'm a rioting mob." Then he desperately begged Jesus not to banish *them.* A large herd of pigs was browsing and rooting on a nearby hill. *The demons* begged him, "Send us to the pigs so we can live in them."
>
> Jesus gave the order. But it was even worse for the pigs than for the man. Crazed, they stampeded over a cliff into the

> sea and drowned. Those tending the pigs, scared to death, bolted and told their story in town and country. Everyone wanted to see what had happened. They came up to Jesus and saw the madman sitting there wearing decent clothes and making sense, no longer a walking madhouse of a man (Mark 5:1-15 MSG)

Musak, in chapter 16 of this book was once possessed by the demon of lust. He cried to God for help, and he was delivered from his demon. What are your demons? Have you tried everything, but nothing seems to help? Call on the name of Jesus for your deliverance. But perhaps you want God to help you but you don't know how to go about it. So, here's a starter.

How can I have a relationship with God?

1. Confess your sins to God (Romans 3:10, 23; 5:12).
2. Ask that the blood of Jesus will cleanse you from all your sins (Hebrew 9:22, 1John 1:7-9).
3. Ask Jesus to come and reign in your life.
4. Forgive yourself and move on:
   Therefore, if anyone is in Christ [that is, grafted in, joined to Him by faith in Him as Savior], he is a new creature [reborn and renewed by the Holy Spirit]; the old things [the previous moral and spiritual condition] have passed away. Behold, new things have come [because spiritual awakening brings a new life] (2 Corinthians 5:17 AMP)
5. Read your Bible and pray every day.
6. Pray that God will lead you to a Bible-believing church and fellowship with them.

Prayer

Lord Jesus, I come to you today; save me and I shall be saved. Heal me and I shall be healed. Forgive me of all my sins (confess them). Have mercy on me. Come and be the Lord over my spirit, soul, and body. Help me not to go back to my old way of life—give me a new beginning. I am yours Lord! In Jesus's name I pray. Amen.

22

To the Parents and Family of People Struggling with Alcohol and Illicit Substance Abuse

If you're tormented by thoughts that you're partly responsible for your child's lifestyle, stop beating yourself up! We all make mistakes; however, two wrongs can never make a right. You may not have raised your child well, and as a result you allow guilt to rule your life. Perhaps you just lacked the knowledge, or you didn't have the right tools or support system. You need to put an end to your guilt. Forgive yourself and be kind to yourself. You didn't know any other way back then. Your little girl or boy is no longer a child. They're young adults or adults now. Adults make decisions. You need to remember you don't have control over your adult child's behaviour. If they've chosen a destructive path despite your warnings, it's on them, not on you. Don't obsess over their condition and try to overcompensate for your mistakes or enable them. That will not help them in any way. Don't reward bad behaviour! This is where you have to use tough love.

Even if you did everything right and you ask yourself repeatedly, "What did I do wrong?" know you didn't do anything wrong. There are certain things in this life that we may never have an answer for. This is one of them. You did your part as a parent. You did all you could. The onus now lies with your child.

That's not to say there's nothing you can do. You can help them in these ways:

- Educate yourself about addiction.
- Get a Naloxone kit if their addiction is opioids or an illegal substance.[43]
- Pray for them.
- Check in on them.
- Send them to rehab.
- Seek counsel.
- Don't enable them or sponsor their bad habits.

You also need to look after yourself. Don't fight your emotions. It's okay to express them in a healthy way. However, it's crucial to manage them. It's equally important to manage your expectations. What you see in your child from time to time may not be what you expected. Some ways to cope include, but are not limited to, talking to a professional and joining a support group. Be positive and hopeful, and whatever you do, don't give up.[44] Check the appendix for a lengthier list of resources.

---

43 Families for Addiction Recovery, "Support Yourself," Retrieved May 18, 2022, from https://www.farcanada.org/family-support/support-yourself/

44 Families for Addiction Recovery, "Support Yourself," Retrieved May 18, 2022, from https://www.farcanada.org/family-support/support-yourself/

23

Where's Bayonle Now?

Bayonle lives in Canada with her family. She's a minister of the gospel and uses her social media platforms to share the message of salvation, joy, hope, peace, healing, and deliverance. She is also a volunteer chaplain at the local correctional centre. She's married to her best friend and partner in the Christianity race, Funso (John) Oderinde. They have been married for over twenty-two years and are parents to two young adults, Isaac and Esther. Bayonle is a nurse clinician; at the time of this writing, she's an enterostomal therapist educator, also known as a nurse specialized in wound ostomy and continence. Although she's not a university professor as she envisioned growing up, as an educator, she teaches her patients and their families about the importance of being responsible for their own health. She affirms that health promotion and disease prevention should be taken seriously. Prevention is better and cheaper than any cure. She also works as a clinical coordinator with the Saskatchewan Health Authority.

By the way, Bayonle is the author of this book! My mother named me Bayonle Olubunmi, and my baptismal name is Eunice. I could have died by suicide during my teenage or early adult years had I given in to my suicidal thoughts. I wanted the end to come so badly. Even worse, I could have lost my mind, become a wanderer or a zombie of sorts. Thankfully, I found

Jesus. If my life had ended at fifteen or eighteen, you wouldn't be reading this book, further proof that you never know what God has in store for you, no matter how hard life gets. I became resilient by relying on the healing power of God. I didn't shut down people who reached out to me genuinely and I allowed God-sent people to help me. I embraced help whenever God brought people into my life. And finally, I learned to lean on people I can trust, such as Agnes, Mrs. Olusola, my pastors in college, and Funso, my husband.

Funso and I agreed early on that we would not raise our children the way we were raised. I want to have a good relationship with my children such that they can open up to me about anything, without fear of being judged or beaten. The bottom line is I don't want history to repeat itself. I want to protect my children, but I know I have to strike a balance in order to avoid being a helicopter parent.

Nonetheless, because of my mommy issues growing up, I knew I would not allow history to repeat itself. So while I'm not a helicopter mom (at least I consciously try not to be) I'm an active mother to my children. I'm not only present physically, but also emotionally and spiritually.

When I remember my childhood trauma, it no longer feels like they're acute or chronic wounds. They're now scars that remind me that I'm strong and resilient. I look at my scars and give thanks to God for giving me hope, joy, peace, and a godly family. I use my scars to serve others because for reasons I don't fully understand, people always seem to come to me with their problems.

So recently, I decided to pursue a master's degree in marriage and family therapy so I can help children, parents, individuals, couples, and families manage their challenges at a professional level. I'm passionate about helping victims and survivors of childhood trauma and parents who have lost their child because I believe I was graced to pass through similar traumas and still be alive to share my story. So now I do my best to comfort others with the comfort I received from the Lord.

This Bible verse sums it up:

> All praise to God, the Father of our Lord Jesus Christ. God is our merciful Father and the source of all comfort. He comforts us in all our troubles so that we can comfort others. When they are troubled, we will be able to give them the same comfort God has given us (2 Corinthians 1:34 NLT).

Life is full of hope. Life is full of choices. Life is full of light. You too can brighten your life and your future. I'll leave you with this, my favourite story:

> When I turned forty in 2015, I asked my family to watch *Barney and Friends* with me, one of my children's favourite TV series when they were younger. I wanted to give my inner child a treat. My favourite part of the show is the final song. That day, as Barney sang that song, tears poured from my eyes like waterfall.
>
> "I love you. You love me.
> We're as happy as can be.
> With a great big hug
> And a kiss from me to you,
> Won't you say you love me too?"[45]

45 Bates Baltes, Stephen, Philip A. Parker, Joseph K. Phillips, and Robert D. Singleton. "Barney Theme Song." *Barney's Favorites, Volume 1.*

My husband and the children jumped up then, wrapped their arms around me, and sang Barney's final song with her. It was so therapeutic!

That was the best birthday ever! And I know the reason I love Barney and children's shows so much—and get teary-eyed at that one song—is partly because I didn't watch cartoons growing up. So now, I watch them whenever I can not only because I like to relive the childhood I wish I'd had, but Barney's final song is a reminder of the love I'm surrounded with now. You too can hang on and overcome!

Sony/ATV Music Publishing LLC and ACUM Ltd. 1993.

References

American Academy of Child and Adolescent Psychiatry. "Physical Punishment." No. 105. Updated March 2018. https://www.aacap.org/AACAP/Families_and_Youth/Facts_for_Families/FFF-Guide/Physical-Punishment-105.aspx

Bates Baltes, Stephen, Philip A. Parker, Joseph K. Phillips, and Robert D. Singleton. "Barney Theme Song." Barney's Favorites, Volume 1. Sony/ATV Music Publishing LLC and ACUM Ltd. 1993.

Burke Harris, Nadine. "How Childhood Trauma Effects Health Across a Lifetime." New York Association of Psychiatric Rehabilitation, Inc. September 9, 2014. https://www.nyaprs.org/e-news-bulletins/2015/ted-childhood-trauma-and-health-across-a-lifetime-and-the-public-health-response-necessary#:~:text=In%20the%20words%20of%20Dr,people%2C%20that's%20a%20terrifying%20prospect

Cherry, Kendra. "Abraham Maslow Quotes about Psychology." ThoughtCo. Updated February 24, 2019. Abraham Maslow Quotes About Psychology (thoughtco.com)

Child Exploitation and Online Protection Centre (CEOP). "Why don't children tell their parents about sexual abuse?" Retrieved May 18, 2022, from https://www.thinkuknow.co.uk/parents/articles/Why-dont-children-tell-their-parents-about-sexual-abuse/

Leaf C (April 27, 2022). "Are you waiting till the "right" moment when you're finally "done" healing to do something?" Facebook Post. Retrieved May 28/22 from https://m.facebook.com/story.php?story_fbid=pfbid-

02A6mKt2tQzaZPz94QEMGMBeV5YDpnYRg-Gx5nzBX3EGPsjyXwYaKABVkLgN7nJoB9N-l&id=100044135541243

Dweck, Carol. S. Mindset: The New Psychology of Success. Ballantine Books, 2007. Penguin Random House Digital, Inc., 2016. https://www.penguinrandomhouse.com/books/44330/mindset-by-carol-s-dweck-phd/

Elliott, B. J., and M. P. Richards. "Effects of parental divorce on children." Archives of Disease in Childhood, 66, no. 8 (1991): 915.

Evans, Darrell. "I'm Trading my Sorrows." Integrity's Hosanna! Music. Divine Hymns. Retrieved May 19, 2022, from https://divinehymns.com/lyrics/im-trading-my-sorrows-song-lyrics/

Families for Addiction Recovery. "Support Yourself." Retrieved May 18, 2022, from https://www.farcanada.org/family-support/support-yourself/

Fergusson, David M., Geraldine F. H. McLeod, and L. John Horwood. "Childhood sexual abuse and adult developmental outcomes: Findings from a 30-year longitudinal study in New Zealand." Child Abuse & Neglect, 37, no. 9 (2013): 664-674. Childhood sexual abuse and adult developmental outcomes: Findings from a 30-year longitudinal study in New Zealand

Francis, Lucine, DePriest, Kelli, Wilson, Marcela, and Gross, Deborah. "Child Poverty, Toxic Stress, and Social Determinants of Health: Screening and Care Coordination." The Online Journal Of Issues In Nursing, 23, no. 3 (2018): 2. https://doi.org/10.3912/OJIN.Vol23No03Man02)

Garon, Risa. "Holiday Time for Children of Divorce." Huffpost. Updated December 18, 2016. https://www.huffpost.

com/entry/holiday-time-for-children_b_8832504

Government of Canada. "Opioid and Stimulant-related Harms in Canada." Updated June 2022. https://health-infobase.canada.ca/substance-related-harms/opioids-stimulants/

Hartney, Elizabeth. "9 Reasons the Cycle of Abuse Continues." Verywell Mind. Updated February 16, 2022. https://www.verywellmind.com/the-cycle-of-sexual-abuse-22460

"Hood." Merriam-Webster Dictionary. Retrieved May 24, 2022, from https://www.merriam-webster.com/dictionary/hood

Kirk, David S. "A natural experiment on residential change and recidivism: Lessons from hurricane Katrina." American Sociological Review, 74, no. 3 (June 2009): 484-505. Retrieved May 23, 2022, from https://www.proquest.com/scholarly-journals/natural-experiment-on-residential-change/docview/218829721/se-2?accountid=50383

Kong, Xiangna, and Wang, Shengyang. "The Relationship between Interparental Conflict Perception and Inferiority Complex of Junior School Students." In Proceedings of the 2016 International Conference on Advances in Management, Arts and Humanities Science. Taiwan-Taichung, December 10–11, 2016, 519522. Atlantis Press, 2016. Retrieved February 12, 2022, from https://www.atlantis-press.com/proceedings/amahs-16/25865871

Mastering Law of Attraction. "The Law of Attraction." Facebook. May 14, 2022. https://www.facebook.com/masteringlawofattraction/

Morton, Kate. The Clockmaker's Daughter. Goodreads. Retrieved from https://www.goodreads.com/quotes/9575478-no-matter-what-evil-might-come-one-

s-way-to-be
Mosel, Stacy. "Brain Damage from Drugs & Alcohol (Are Effects Reversible?)." American Addiction Centers. Edited by Amelia Sharp. Updated May 20, 2022. https://americanaddictioncenters.org/alcoholism-treatment/brain-damage
Motivation Posters. "A Reason A Season and A Lifetime." Retrieved from https://motivationposters.com/index.php?route=product/product&product_id=367
Munroe, Miles. Understanding Your Potential: Discovering the Hidden You. Shippensburg, PA: Destiny Image Publishers, 2011.
Myles Munroe. The Wealthy Place Cemetery. Video file. August 5, 2021. The Wealthy Place Cemetery - Dr. Myles Munroe - YouTube
Nielsen, Linda. "How Dads Affect Their Daughters into Adulthood." Institute for Family Studies. Updated June 3, 2014. https://ifstudies.org/blog/how-dads-affect-their-daughters-into-adulthood#:~:text=An%20emerging%20body%20of%20research,with%20their%20dads%20during%20childhood.
Noll, Jennie G., Penelope K. Trickett, William W. Harris, and Frank W. Putnam. (2009). "The Cumulative Burden Borne by Offspring Whose Mothers Were Sexually Abused as Children: Descriptive Results From A Multigenerational Study." Journal of Interpersonal Violence, 24, no. 3 (March 2009.): 424–449. National Library of Medicine. https://doi.org/10.1177/0886260508317194
Oderinde, Eunice. Blog. Deliverance Prayers. Retrieved May 23, 2022, from https://euniceoderinde.blogspot.com/2021/09/deliverance-prayers.html
Pace, Rachael. "How a Lack of Communication in Mar-

riage can Affect Relationships." Marriage.com Updated November 20, 2020. https://www.marriage.com/advice/communication/lack-of-communication-in-marriage/

"Preserve." Merriam-Webster Dictionary. Retrieved May 24, 2002, from https://www.merriam-webster.com/dictionary/preserve

"Prevent." Merriam-Webster Dictionary. Retrieved May 24, 2022, from https://www.merriam-webster.com/dictionary/prevent

"Protect." Merriam-Webster Dictionary. Retrieved May 24, 2022, from https://www.merriam-webster.com/dictionary/protect

Rappaport, S.R. "Deconstructing the Impact of Divorce on Children." Family Law Quarterly, 47, no. 3 (2013): 353-377.

Ritchie, Hannah, and Max Roser. "Drug Use." Our World In Data. Retrieved May 11, 2022, from https://ourworldindata.org/drug-use

Schmidt, Courtney. "How and why to talk to your kids about their private parts." Orlando Health, Arnold Palmer Hospital for Children. March 29, 2018. https://www.arnoldpalmerhospital.com/content-hub/how-and-why-to-talk-to-your-kids-about-their-private-parts

Segrin, Chris. "Social skills deficits associated with depression." Clinical Psychology Review, 20, no. 3 (April 2000): 379-403. Retrieved May 18, 2022, from https://www.sciencedirect.com/science/article/abs/pii/S0272735898001044

SickKids Staff. "Sexuality: what children should learn and why." SickKids. Retrieved May 23, 2022 from https://www.aboutkidshealth.ca/Article?contentid=716&language=English#:~:text=Pre%2Dteens%3A%20Nine%20

to%2012,sexually%20transmitted%20infections%20(STIs)

Towns, Elmer. "Is God Fair to Answer the Prayers of Some People and Not Others?" In Ten Questions about Prayer Every Christian Must Answer, 33–45. Nashville, TN: B&H Publishing Group, 1999. Ten Questions about Prayer Every Christian Must Answer (liberty.edu)

Women of Faith. "I'm Trading My Sorrows." YouTube video. Uploaded February 17, 2012. May 19, 2022, https://www.youtube.com/watch?v=4K1jnnz0skQ

Watkins-Kagebein, Jennifer, Barnett, T. M., Collier-Tenison, S., and Blakey, J. "They Don't Listen: A Qualitative Interpretive Meta-Synthesis of Children's Sexual Abuse." Child and Adolescent Social Work Journal, 36, no. 4 (August 15, 1999): 337-349.

Watson, Stephanie, and Kristeen Cherney. "Effects of Sleep Deprivation." Healthline Media. Updated December 15, 2021. https://www.healthline.com/health/sleep-deprivation/effects-on-body

APPENDIX

Resources for Victims of Childhood Trauma and their Parents/Guardians and Loved Ones

1. Wall Foundation: Nigeria https://wallfoundations.org/
2. Mirabel Centre: Nigeria https://mirabelcentre.org/
3. Canada Centre for Child Protection https://www.protectchildren.ca/en/resources-research/survivors/
4. Help for Adult Victims of Child Abuse https://www.havoca.org/
5. I am Praise Fowowe International https://www.iampraisefowowe.com/
6. The Cumulative Burden Borne by Offspring Whose Mothers Were Sexually Abused as Children https://journals.sagepub.com/doi/10.1177/0886260508317194
7. Child Exploitation and Online Protection Centre (CEOP): UK https://www.thinkuknow.co.uk/parents/
8. Ending Violence Association of Canada https://endingviolencecanada.org/sexual-assault-centres-crisis-lines-and-support-services/
9. The Enough Abuse Campaign: USA https://www.enoughabuse.org/
10. Sungatekids USA https://sungatekids.org/
11. Child Custody topics Divorce Canada https://divorce-canada.ca/child-custody-in-canada
12. Abuse Survivor Resources: USA & Canada https://isurvive.org/helpful-resources/abuse-survivor-resources-usa-canada/
13. Mental Health Commission of Canada https://mentalhealthcommission.ca/

14. Government of Canada; Get Help with Substance Use https://www.canada.ca/en/health-canada/services/substance-use/get-help-problematic-substance-use.html
15. Families for Addiction Recovery: Canada https://www.farcanada.org/

Made in the USA
Middletown, DE
14 October 2024

62653346R00109